BlAcKpOeMoLoGy

Men of Colour In Transitory Stages: (A Choreopoem)
- Pseudo Autobiographical - Tragicomedy!

david vincent brooks

authorHOUSE®

AuthorHouse™
1663 Liberty Drive
Bloomington, IN 47403
www.authorhouse.com
Phone: 1-800-839-8640

Published by AuthorHouse 6/7/2013

ISBN: 978-0-7596-6839-3 (sc)
ISBN: 978-0-7596-6838-6 (e)

Any people depicted in stock imagery provided by Thinkstock are models, and such images are being used for illustrative purposes only. Certain stock imagery © Thinkstock.

This book is printed on acid-free paper.

Because of the dynamic nature of the Internet, any web addresses or links contained in this book may have changed since publication and may no longer be valid.

The views expressed in this work are solely those of the author and do not necessarily reflect the views of the publisher, and the publisher hereby disclaims any responsibility for them.

ACT I...

Movements in time...Man-to-Man Relationships

BEFORE...(slave trade to mid-50s)

>The bible says men help "form" each other: "*As iron sharpens iron, so a man sharpens his friends.*" (**Proverbs 27:17**)

(**Overture**: "**Ancestral Call**" by Jay U Xperíence. The stage is dark and quiet for the moment. A man & a woman appears center stage in a spot light fully dressed in African attire; resembling royalty. Later, that man & woman are stripped to peasant clothing and sold on an auction block. All of a sudden, there's a flash of light, and screams are heard somewhere from off stage. People are running, screaming in what appears to be a state of frenzy...then silence, once again. Man in black emerges from audience and steps into a dim light—which appears center stage. It seems, as if all of a sudden panic has taken over him... yet upon seeing the audience he begins to relax...more screams are heard from off stage...the lights come up, and suddenly the audience sees masses of bodies laying on the stage floor in what appears to be chains and torn sheets...the interior resembles a slave ship, that has landed somewhere in the Virginia territory, during or around the time of the slave trade...In 1841, when the day before, a slaveship called Creole left Hampton, Va., for New Orleans...only to experience a revolt by the slaves on board. Later, Great Britain grants them asylum and set them free in various parts of Nassau, Bahamas. This story is about the slaves who remain in Virginia in 1841...and later moved beyond and toward the North and or other parts of the world—preparing themselves for the new millennium).

Note: the () indicates the next poetic monologue and/or other directions for the men or woman throughout this entire choreopoem. In addition, thoughout the entire performance there's a hugh screen that projects images of city streets, parks, buildings and wooded areas and images of famous and not so famous people.

BEFORE...

(Man wearing black...standing center stage, suddenly starts to speak directly to the audience. All of the other men are shirtless. They are wearing black slacks and laying on the floor...the man wearing black is the narrator & protector of them all. The man wearing black is screaming "Sikiliza (listen in swahili) to the other men and woman. One man yells "Nisaidie" (help), then all the other people start yelling "Nisaidie." The man wearing black, yells "Simameni! (stop in swahili)" & everyone stops & he looks out towards the audience and his comrades—then the man wearing black starts speaking, again...while the woman starts tending to each individual man...caring for their wounds and preparing their "souls" for some discomfort ahead. She begins to dress them in their new clothing. Their new garments represents each man's color (sort of a coat-of-armor). The woman helps each man get dressed; except for one man who remains in bondage. Later, that same man becomes the man wearing purple...)

(Prelude)

...for you/   (Man wearing black)
the new world/the promised land/
here are some: empty, blank, lily white stones.../hot, spicy & tasty dishes.../
dried, crusty, ole bloodstained clothed patches/broken dreams/
torn/ripped, outdated/& very much ole faded photograph' of year' passed.../

                    (Man wearing black throws down a couple of photo...)

these things/I leave for you...

I

...on a hot spring day/   (Man wearing green rises from the floor speaking,
a spring day/   while putting on his shirt)
in the month of/

                                                        (what is now called May)

I dreamt.../I dreamt/I'd swam across the Mediterranean Sea & landed...

I dreamt/   (Man wearing white rises from the floor speaking...)
I landed/upon/
the mainstream of homemade apple pie & french vanilla ice cream/
then/I/was forced to dress up in drab & insipid colours...

colours of:
Red, White & Blue   (Man wearing white looks over at the other two men who
                                         will later become those very same coloures...)

colours/   (Man wearing beige rises from floor speaking...
that contrast/   "Going Back to My Roots" by Odyssey
with/   is heard in the background)
my ancestral natural colours/of:
blue black & indigo blue.../

II

(Man wearing blue rises from floor speaking...)

I then/
headed further North or was it South?/
or maybe the Far East?/Oh, my God, for sure I am now completely lost!!!/

lost/   (Man wearing brown rises from floor speaking)
as I continue to look for/
the promise land.../
the promise land.../
the promise land.../

for you see/   (Man wearing orange rises from floor speaking)
time had passed/& now I find myself/
on some crowded vessel.../
a vessel/you/described as being/fit for a king

while/   (Man wearing red rises from floor speaking)
waving your flag & banner/
of stars & stripes/which was stitched together by some animal/

from what i've later learned/was a representative of some Borden's product
called Betsy' the cow/

I'd   (Man wearing purple rises speaking)
also learned to turn cartwheels/
& perform some wild/& amazing somersaults/while standing on something/
(once again)/you called, being fit for a king.../
of which i've again learned/was called an auction block!

(Man wearing beige runs over sizing the Man in purple up, as if he was a slave owner)

standing there/   (Man in purple continues speaking-sort of embarrassed)
on your God forsaken auction block.../
just a grinning/& not one grin was ever returned back!/
as if.../as if I was invisible.../

invisible/except for the gleaming of my pearly white.../pearly white teeth
as you continued to probe my mouth & genitals/with your fingers...

(Women turns her head in shame...while handing the man a purple shirt)

I then, too/   *(Man wearing black starts to speak)*
became madder/
madder than a mad-hatter!/my emotions stirring/my emotions boiling/
as a matter of fact/hotter than some Salem Witches poisonous brew/

don't/   *(Man wearing red rushing in, cutting the man in black off...repeats*
you know who I am?/   *himself twice, before being cut off by man wearing brown)*
I/   *(Man wearing brown...cutting off man wearing red)*
am the dark prince/
called Baye (Bay-yah)/straight forward/& of an West African King/
Khary (Car-ree)/who was Kingly in Senegal & Gambia/

my sister/   *(Man wearing blue)*
name is Assata (Ah-sah-tah)/she's a warrior, too!/

my brother/   *(Man wearing green)*
Idrissa (Eee-dree-sah)/is immortal/you fool!!!/

            (Man wearing green is directly addressing the audience)

for sure/you must realized, that you are declaring war!/

kidnappin' me from my Motherland.../   *(Man wearing black)*
Fatou Mata (Fah-too-mah-tah)/
I was beloved by all who knew me.../

III

now/   *(Man wearing beige...pantomiming the act of joggling balls)*
i'm juggling colorful/
bouncy balls & acting the court jester/

do you know who I am?/   *(Man wearing white)*

Baye! Baye! Baye!/   *(Everyone shouts out)*

I...am...a...a.../   *(Man wearing black)*
Dark Prince/& while you sat down/
& wrote letters to a newly elected city hall/

I was gagged/   (Man wearing orange)
beaten in & out of my blackness/
& chained to your slave ships/
& threaten to be put to my death!!!/

I didn't escaped/   (Man wearing yellow)
yet/somehow/
I managed to employ/
your independence on the 4th of July in 1776.../

IV

I was there/   (Man wearing black)
when against the Declaration of Independence/
in Rochester, New York/Frederick Douglass/
a distant relation of mine/read his rebuttal/
in your very own language titled: "I Hear The Mournful Wait of Millions..."/

V

I/   (Man wearing yellow cutting off man wearing black)
believe, my brother.../
that was the summer of 1852/
& the title was "The Meaning of July Fourth for The Negro...,"/
on the same white stoned steps/
that/formed a massive building (which my people built)/
while surrounded by unhappy/& bitter white faces...

seeing their faces/   (Man wearing beige jumps up)
made me shout for joy!/

shout for joy/   (Man wearing blue)
over brother Douglass' strength/

shout for joy/   (Man wearing green)
over brother Douglass blackness/
& the knowledge/that/I am Baye! Baye!/
straight forward/for you'll never know how so.../

for I am still waiting/   (Man wearing black)
for South Africa today.../
my ancestral homeland/to regain her very own/
Independence/

(Stage lights dim down to a fade...but no one exits from the stage,
while remaining motionless until the very end)

after having watched/
your every move America...

(   )

ocean, oh! ocean/   (Lights come up and man wearing white starts to speak)
rushing in & rushing out/
as the years go by/i wonder what little secrets you may have in store to tell?/

for centuries mankind have used you/   (Man in beige)
for wars & long voyages/many men/
from aristocrats to slaves have felt your cruelty/

I for one know/   (Man wearing white)
the ecstasy of walking along the sea shores/
& watching the tides & waves/doing their dance to your sea haunting sounds/

your ocean floors/   (Man wearing beige)
are covered with so much history.../
history of collectors items.../
items from jewels to ancient cities ruins/

in the beginning.../
God's spirit moved upon the surface of the raging seas/
then commanded every.../every drop to become peacefully still!/

Moses as a child/floated upon the Nile/Moses as a Man/
stepped upon the Red Sea & by the grace of God/
he parted the way.../parted the way for his people to be set free.../

ocean, oh ocean/   (Man wearing white)
without you/my life will be in great danger/
so as long as you keep flowing/I know/
that my life through you can expect/
New Horizon...

(*Men wearing beige & white exits together down stage right*)

(*Lights dim down only, while two spot lights appear on Men wearing black & red. In the background is the image of a hanging noose-a small group of people appear—resembling a lynching mob. The time is in the mid 20s, 30s or maybe even the 40s...A time of continued racism & jim crowism*)

(   )

I

a certain wind blew my way the other day/   (*Man wearing red*)

a strange sort of wind/   (*Man wearing black*)
a wind of unhappy times/

times of ropes/   (*Man wearing red*)
times of chains/
times of blood stained broken tree branches/
& hot tar/& white chicken feather's/

a fowl stench/   (*Man wearing black*)
a stench of his unforgotten sweetness/
sweetness turned bitter/& his pain/which caught some by surprise.../
& had become tied up like a knot/at the center of their waistline/
& as they all stood there/
& watched his body tossed about the blood soaked grounds.../

while he/   (*Man wearing red*)
in this stiff stance...started twirling & twirling/
& casting a murky aura over their ghoulish little heads.../
under the elm/or was it an oak tree?/

II

the women folk/   (*Man wearing blue emerges & starts to speak;*)
made/their way/   (*along with the woman*)
through the crowd/   (*The woman ad lib the following:*)
front line/   "*Excuse me...pardon me...etc., etc.,*")
& center crying out loud: "*Why, dear Lord, why...*"/   (*Woman screams out*)

(*Man wearing green speak, while all the other men lower their heads...in shame*)

the men/
as usual/
bowed their bald/& or nappy heads/in shame/while/clinching their fists/

as the children/   (Man wearing black)
continued to play/

        (Ad lib: Other men & woman sings some muffled children's nursery rhyme)

as/   (Man wearing red)
if they/had not a care in the world/
did they really think/those hooded white sheets/
had a resemblance to some friendly ghost?/

III

a certain wind blew my way/   (Man wearing black)
the other day/then came the pouring rain/
mixed with salty tears/dried up from the days bright sunlight...

for over the past couple of years/we have once again/   (Man wearing red)
finally come to recall/that windy day/as/the day/
the ole man/who/some folk said:
had such a gentle sweetness...a gentle spirit.../
died/beneath my grandaddy's/backyard elm/or was it/an oak tree.../

    (Man wearing blue exit slowly, while looking over his shoulder center stage left toward the
    man wearing red, who's standing center stage, staring at the swing noose as "Strange Fruit"
    is heard faintly from off stage...men in black & green joins the man wearing red, and they
    all start clenching their fist's, while pounding their right thighs...lights dim to a fade)

(This poem can be omitted for brevity...)

      (Men wearing black, blue & orange enters into one of the three spotlights
        on stage, then man wearing orange starts to speaks)

the in's & out's/of stayin' black/like being-in-love/
ain't no way one can turn back.../

yet tea is served w/cream/   (Man wearing blue)
& all God's lil black chillus may have their own dreams/

dreams of mama's/   (Man wearing black)
running faucet/

dreams of papa's/   (Man wearing orange)
escorting himself/up life's DeAd EnD cReEk/
w/out a mothership/

or/   (Man wearing blue)
a promise land to look back upon/

now/   (Man wearing black, addressing the audience &
let's see/   the other men on stage with him)
you try to swim back to Congo?/

black skin a burning/   (Man wearing orange)
bones a crackling/
neck is rapping w/life's forbidden noose/
& their goes/
another black chin swinging from LiMb to LiMb/   (Once again the hangin' noose
                                                      appears, only to disappear)

tryin' to pick forbidden fruits/   (Man wearing blue)
that isn't quite just ripe/
only leaves a BiTtEr TaStE/
of what seems like life's SwEeT dElIgHt/

golden melons/   (Man wearing orange)
in dainty lil patches/

oil burner's/   (Man wearing black)
that aren't yet matching/
the nights skylight/

the shadows of granddaddy/   (Man wearing blue)
dirty old bible/hangin' from his overall back pocket/

in the-wee-small-hours of the night/   (Man wearing black)
we sat & listen to stories of cotton-fields/
& hog scraps/that help strengthen/all God's lil black chillus backs...
while carryin' white cotton on their dirty black backs/

while/   (Man wearing orange)
riding in the mist of all this commotion/

i wonder what things would have been like/
if mama & papa/papa & mama/mama & papa/weren't stolen & brought/
to this here promise land.../of broken dreams/broken languages/
broken spirits.../
& broken souls.../   (Lights fade out...everyone exists...only to reappear)

            (Entire cast enters stage from various stage entrances chanting "Go home...")

(This poem can be omitted for brevity...)

go home/   (In unison)

            (Man wearing black speaks...while everyone else tires to cuts him off before he can finish)

fuck you!/

no, go home/   (In unison)

no, fuck you!/   (Man wearing black)

can you?/   (In unison)

your mama!/   (Man wearing black)

say what?/go home/   (In unison)

where's home?/   (Man wearing black)

South Africa!/   (In unison)

oh, no, no, no, way.../they killing nig.../over there/in South Africa, too!/
                        (Man wearing black stops using the "N" word in mid-sentence)

hell/wez shooting nig.../i'ze mean negros/& negros/
are shooting each other/
over here, too!...   (Man wearing red catches himself using the "N" word)

say what?/   (Everyone...looking around the stage & out to the audience.)

go home!/   (Man wearing red)

I guess wez/
better be heading for home.../   (Man wearing black exit stage right with his head
                                           bowed down...lights dim and the remaining cast exists.)

(   )

I

the walls/   (Man wearing green starts speaking)
the bricks/the men/the women/
their children/& their children's/
children/are all our children.../

II

now days/   (Man wearing white)
lover's walk through city parks/
that used to be landmarks of slave owners.../
slave owners who sold/their mama & papa/

yesterday/   (Man wearing yellow)
I heard a preacher/preaching the gospel/
on a busy city street/tears suddenly appeared...

once I'd remember/   (Man wearing green)
my people of long ago/my people/
who had to speak in codes/of one day finding/
freedom upon this here promise land/

today'/   (Man wearing white)
young people/black people/
thinkin' of lust/rather than/lovin' one another.../
4 u see 2 many of our children/are having children of their own.../

haven't we already paid the cost?/   (Man wearing yellow)

we/   (Man wearing green)
need to take time to read/to talk/
to in better ourselves/then/perhaps/we can tear down these walls.../
& use the remaining bricks/to help build up a mighty people!/

III

many nations/   *(Man wearing white)*
have watched/the South Africans apatheid system/
calling it anything/but what it is.../modern day oppression/
yet/remaining mentally under a yoke.../isn't a joke/
unless one can find humor in b-r-o-k-e-n window panes
& burning crosses/
upon America's very own green grass.../   *(All three men dash off stage)*

(   )

        (A few men enters the stage carrying suitcases and other loaded bags, boxes etc., etc.
              The men are brown, purple and orange. The man in orange starts to speak)

a bus ride into the city/can make one feel kind of silly/

Rosa's in the park/   *(Man wearing purple)*
& yet she couldn't sit on the front of a blasted bus/

she became red in the face/   *(Man wearing brown)*
black rooted to the core/while everyone else/
was lily white & bitter/

yet/   *(Man wearing purple)*
Ms. Rosa/
managed to get a front row seat/
with/the help from a young man.../a young man by the name.../
Dr. Martin Luther King/

for one's/   *(Man wearing orange)*
dark history is forgivable/
but/never forgotten/

no/   *(Man wearing brown)*
matter the time.../

no/   *(Man wearing purple)*
matter the era.../

the first hand is always movin'/   *(Man wearing orange)*
& tryin' to catch up too/
what the second hand is doin'/

whether an hour/   *(Man wearing brown)*
a day/or year…a bus ride into the city/
can make one feel might silly/

then/   *(Man wearing purple)*
why do some folks/
continue to ride off to far off places/
on the back of modern day buses/
& still call themselves niggers?/   *(All three man slowing starts to exit stage left)*

(   )

it all started out/   *(Enters man wearing blue…he starts speaking to the audience)*
with/
one tear in the corner of one's eye/
than/it went on to becoming/
the haunting sounds of a newborn baby's stomach growlin'/
growlin' from hungry/
afterwards/we all could see/that/
America once again/
played the charitable nation/
it is well noted for…/

(   )

      (All the men enter the stage, while joining the man wearing blue from various volms, and
         hustling, pantomiming con games on a busy city street. Man in black starts to speak)

for you see…over the past few years/
two hundred & twenty-two years/to be exact/

the United States/   *(Man wearing beige)*
has involved itself/
in virtually every corner of the world/

but not my corner of 125th Street/   *(Man wearing red)*

hands across America/   *(Man wearing black)*
& freedom marches/
with protest songs about freein'/
whales & savin' the rain forest/

but/   (Man wearing red)
not one damn finger/not one damn foot print/
not one damn voice/
was lifted past my corner of 125th Street.../

yet/   (Man wearing beige)
America/
is still called a democracy by some/& some seems to think/
it's more like a place/where the elitist shall meet/
then/decide what, where, how & who everyone else shall eat/
sleep with, vote for...& or even fuck!/

                    (*A shock reaction shows from the other men...*)

the free lunches/   (Man wearing black)
the after school programs/the summer youth jobs/
but/not a damn one stayed/
for long on my corner of 125th street.../

                (*All the men dashes off stage...through various volms*)

(   )

I'd/   (*Enters men in orange, brown & green...man in green starts to speak.*)
left NYC/
& headed straight for interstate 95/

I/   (Man wearing brown)
left NYC/
for a taste of adventure/

I managed/   (Man wearing green)
to get/as far as the Mason Dixie line/
& had a strange revelation.../

a revelation/   (Man wearing orange)
of tall green grass/that/
had always looked fresher on the other side/
of my Jim crow boarded up fences/

but/   (Man wearing brown)
once you step over & beyond/
there you go again/steppin' into the same ole shit/

(16)   BlAcKpOeMoLoGy

memories of: (Man wearing green)
apple blossoms/cherry trees/swimmin' holes/
lynching mobs/& po lil ole black boys like me/

I/ (Man wearing orange)
soon forgot/the smell of the vender smelly hands/
in NYC Central Park/

an odor/ (Man wearing brown)
of stale mustard & burnt franks/
foul aroma's/steamin' from the pissy pores of an irish immigrant/
street po' ole vendor/

then I/ (Man wearing green)
recalled the reasons why I'd left NYC/
on the Greyhound bus/listenin' to Billie's Lament "Strange Fruit"/

(The song "Strange Fruit" is vaguely heard from off stage again then the volume dims to a slow fade)

of black bodies/ (Man wearing orange)
twisted mouths/& blood on leaves/

my days turned/ (Man wearing brown)
into dark Georgia nights/as I entered/
the darkness of the deep south/the south of my northern pass/

my throat had become dry/ (Man wearing green)

I/ (Man wearing orange)
felt a burnin' sensation/
as/if there was somethin' circling my neck.../

while/ (Man wearing brown)
menacin' eyes became visible/yet/
from only behind hooded white sheets/
while glancin' back at my black soul/& there was Billie's lament:
"Strange Fruit" playin'somewhere off in the distant night air/

(Once again the same music is heard from off stage to a slow fade)

& my bitter reality/ (Man wearing orange)
had suddenly kicked in/that/
racism has once again/reared it's ugly head/

quickly/   (Man wearing green)
sendin' me back to NYC/
in a wooden unmarked box/

no/   (Man wearing brown)
longer seekin' adventure/for my blood/
now soaked the Georgia' red clay dirt.../

& oh now/   (Man wearing orange)
my spirit roams/
this bitter earth's end/
lookin' for peace/
or sweet revenge.../   (Lights dim and all three men exit stage right)

(   )

the Greyhound bus/   (Enters men wearing red, black & beige/
the Trailways bus/   Man in black starts to speak)
by/now wouldn't one/
think after all these years/a 3rd bus would have shown up?/

poof!/   (Man wearing beige, while the man wearing red looks at him in disgust)
like magic/
here comes Peter Pan!/

u/   (Man wearing black, addressing the audience)
see/i'm in need of a change.../
can you spare some?/

after/   (Man wearing red)
seeing/so many/black & white knights/
Amerika's/true heroines & warrior/from/Lady Day/
Tommy Dorsey & his band/
to Dr. King & Bayard Rustin/leading marches/toward the White House/

dirty roads/   (Man wearing beige speak as he looks over towards the other men)
leading everyone/
across Amerika'/
highways & byways/from Mississippi to DC/
protesting the wrong/
in separating all God's chillus/

whether/   (Man wearing black)
in the back/
or up-front, first or last.../

u/   (Man wearing beige)
see/a change/a change/had to come/

u/   (Man wearing red)
see/colored signs.../
colored signs/
they/didn't last.../   (Man wearing red holds up a picket sign...then tosses it off stage.)

at/   (Man wearing black)
least/
in public domain.../

      (All men exit upper stage right/ except the man in black/who seems lost in thought)

(   )

      (Man wearing black starts to speak once he realizes that all eyes are upon him)

to be somebody/
I/
was brought up in the city/
thinking/white was right/& black.../
well/let's just say.../black was just/
that/
black!/now get back.../

to be somebody/
I/
felt home was no place for me to live/
so/
I left/& now i'm homeless/with a home I can always go back to/
if it weren't for my foolish pride/to be like everyone else/
I/
had to be different & in my differences/
I/
became bitter & resentful of mankind/

to be somebody/
I/
had to lose myself in the light of the morning' brightness/
only to find myself/groping around on all fours/like a dog in the dark/

to be somebody/
I/
guess/I must get use to being bright spirited in such a dark/& indifferent world.../

(Man wearing black exits...down stage left)

(   )

(Enters men wearing red, purple and green from center stage left & right.
Man wearing red starts to speak)

hey, Mr.../
hey, excuse me Sir?/i'm in need of some smoke/
& you offer me a pack of false lies (as if there's a such a thing as truthful lies)/

waking up with the chills & shakes/   (Man wearing purple)
& here you come with/that/Great-White-Milky-Way.../

i've asked for more opportunities/   (Man wearing red)
& you tell me you're considered a minority, too!/
& to hell with affirmative action/
& may the best man of any kind win/

I am sitting next to you/   (Man wearing green)
in Biology class/Chemistry class/
& riding next to you on the IRT, IND/
all the way uptown,/you stopping at 96th Street/
& me at 125th Street/
& secretly you're laughing/smiling/'cause I referred to my manhood/
as my johnson/dick/cock/while you were thinking/
phallus symbols...or the Washington Monument/

in my thinking/   (Man wearing purple)
that A-T-O-M/was the father of mankind/
or man of any kind/
being/He, was the 1st man of God's creation/

according to the WORD!/
& then you tell me/that/I'm spelling/A-D-A-M wrong/

&/
to you/I am just a tiny particle of anything/
but nothing.../you see I come from a very simple background.../
yet it was your institutions/
your institutions...that...that educated me.../
but/   (Man wearing green)
how much longer/shall I continue to turn the other cheek?/

for you see I can't afford.../   (Man wearing red)
I can't afford no plastic face lifts!/

I don't even have a credit card!/   (Man wearing purple)

yeah, men don't cry/   (Man wearing green)
hell, I don't know about all men of any kind,/
but I have cried silent tears/for not only myself/
but for my brother, too!/

& I...as.../   (Man wearing red)
a Blackman.../
I've cried bittersweet tears...\with & for my brother/
when he has to leave a wife with 7 lil mouths to feed/
or was killed by some racist dick/or o.d. on some rat poison/
or may even had to wear a dress/with hairdo to match/
only to make ends meet.../

(Man wearin' red looks over at the man wearing beige...)

than/   (Man wearing green)
I'll have to watch him fight in high heels/
while tryin' to keep the title of being a man/
while on the verge of tears/
& you're making affirmative action jokes.../   (All men exit down stage right...)

(   )

(Enters man wearing white & he starts to speak/while attempting
to be eatin' somethin' from out of a can)

one day/
I/sat myself down for a light lunch/

I/
helped myself…you know…a lil sumthin' sumthin'/
to/a hefty helping of:

       abc's,666,CIA,MIA, pow, FBI, AIDS, even KKK, the NAACP
       & some good ole SNCC got an eyeful of MTV's, WABC, CBS
       & oh, yes my dear PBS trip on some PCP, LSD while reminiscing about JFK…

I than finally had enuf/
& thought to myself…hey…/this was suppose to have been/
a vegetarian dish of just plain ole chicken booth…/

      (Man wearing white throws the can of soup off stage right & exits stage left)

(   )

it's a diverse art/   *(Enter man wearing yellow rubbing is head has he enter*
it…/being the art/   *from stage right)*
the art of shaking hands…you know…/
how are you doing my brother…/my sister/

every/   *(Man wearing yellow, extends his hand out to the audience)*
muscle in one's body/
plays a part in this here rude awakening game/

      (Enter man wearing orange with a damp cloth for his brother' head/
      Both man shake hands/while man wearing orange starts to speak.)

the art of shaking hands/
brings to mind…/brings to mind/
that/
some sort of understanding has been established/
wouldn't/you agree?/

      (Man wearing orange first is speaking to the man wearing yellow…then the audience)

yet/   *(Man wearing yellow)*
wars have been fought/
over the shaking of one's hands/& even worst/
weapons have been sold/

people/   (Man wearing orange)
are bitter in their hearts/& filled with so much hatred/
even/when claiming to be shaking a brother's hand/

only/   (Man wearing yellow)
to find themselves/
needing that same brother' hand in their time of need.../

see/   (Man wearing orange extends his hands out towards the audience)
for yourself/
it's just a hand shake away/

either/   (Man wearing yellow)
you can shake a hand/& make a friend/
or/start another war/
which/one/would you prefer?/

            (Man wearing yellow addresses the audience/both men exit/first towards
            stage right/then remembers the can & chooses to exit stage left instead)

(   )

yes, it has!/   (Enters men wearing blue, beige and white...
yes, it has!/   man wearing white start to speak)
yes, it has!/
yes, it has!/   (All "yes it has" are spoken in unison...)

but/   (Man wearing white)
it never was said like this/
until...now!/

until now.../   (Man wearing blue)

I/   (Man wearing beige)
love/
staying up late all night/
yet/   (Man wearing white)
I hate getting up to greet the morning sun/

I/   (Man wearing beige)
love playing games of chances/

yet/   (Man wearing blue)
I dare you to make one false move/
causing/me to challenge you to a deadly duel/

I/   (Man wearing beige)
love french fries/

I/
love french mustard greens/
&/
I/
love french toast
yet/
the only knowledge of the French language/
that I've learned.../
i've learned from watching/
the American "Bonjour, Bonjour" jeans commercial/

I/   (Man wearing blue)
think it's all been said before/

but/   (Man wearing beige)
I/
think/
I/
should say it again/

I/   (Man wearing white)
should study my adoptive native homeland/
before venturing across to the foreign shores.../Ne ce pas?/

                (In unison...then all three exit center stage left...)

(   )

I/   *(Enters men wearing beige, green, red...Man wearing beige states to speak)*
could/
have been born with a silver spoon in my mouth/
&/ate from life's grandest menu/

I/   (Man wearing green)
could have chosen a different path/
instead of the one I am now traveling.../

(24)   BlAcKpOeMoLoGy

I/   (Man wearing beige)
could have walked/
in my precious bronze childhood booties/
or/continued to suck on my thumb/
like the family photo's in dollar picture frames.../

family/   (Man wearing red)
photo albums/
that/
hold some truth/& stores some lies/

yet/   (Man wearing beige)
proud of being a family heirloom/
was never a choice given to me!/

instead/   (Man wearing red)
I accepted the status/
of being a black sheep/in search of his lil bo peep/
both/of us left out of life's greener pastures/

        (Man wearing beige speaks/while holding up a pair of red high
            heels...man wearing red takes them from him)

& wez all know./
child/
that/
God's children all need a descent pair of get up & go shoes/

while/   (Man wearing red speaks, while throwin' the heels off stage)
it makes no sense/
in sporting bronze booties/when there's three other nappy headed mouths to
feed/

hand-me-downs/   (Man wearing beige...acting as if tryin' on some clothin'.)
was my a childhood/
past time/
I could have/
been a queen/been a prince/been a king

instead/   (Man wearing green, while trying to keep the peace between the other two)
I/
am just a pauper/down on my borrowed luck/

I/   (Man wearing red)
sort plenty/from the goodness of many/
then/
I/
was forced to give it back/

now/   (Man wearing green)
I ain't got much.../
that/
was in the beginning/& the middle ain't looking no brighter!/
My sister' & brother'/

so/   (Man wearing red)
when/the end comes.../

I/   (Man wearing beige, while looking over to man wearing red for forgiveness)
shall expect/
I shall be none/the wiser.../

        (Men wearing green & red exit together/leaving man wearing beige alone...who later exits)

(   )   (Lights come up on men wearing brown, yellow & white)

the record states/clearly/   (Man wearing brown)
that/
if a man cuts himself/he would must surely bleed/

not necessary to death/   (Man wearing yellow)
mind you/but/bleed nevertheless/

it also states/   (Man wearing white)
the/
record that is/
that/
if a man should turn the other cheek/he would for sure/be smart enuf/
to at least/wait/until the other side/heals/before offering the other.../

you/   (Man wearing yellow)
see/
life is a vicious cycle/
waiting to repeat/the shock of knocking/one/
back into a state of reality/even for the second time around/
since/history/does repeat itself/

(26)   BlAcKpOeMoLoGy

a/   (Man wearing brown)
woman/
the record states/is a person/a person who's to remain/voiceless in GOD's house/
yet/
i'm sure without a shadow of a doubt.../that no one/would/ever dare/
to have told that to MAHALIA JACKSON/all praises be!/

Well.../   (Everyone in unison)

the record indicates: (Man wearing white)
we are all our mama's babies/
& daddies maybeeeeees.../
yet/
from listening to LADY DAY singing the BLUES,/
eventually in the end/GOD blesses only the child/
that's/
got his own/can I get an amen?/

Amen.../   (Everyone in unison)

its all a part of growing up/   (Man wearing yellow)
& being on one' own/
a child may or may not state/the entire truth on record/
but/
the truth shall set the lil' liars free/

as if/only there's such a thing as finding truth in one' lies...uhm?/

children/   (Man wearing brown)
we are learning/are taught by their elders.../
the record states/
that/
some elders are like children/than where in the hell does that leave the children?/

children/   (Man wearing white)
who will someday/become/the elders of the next generations/

the record/   (In unison, as each man exit from various exits)
doesn't state/
that.../

(   )   (Enters men wearing orange, blue & purple...purple is eating something?)

I/   (Man wearing blue is speaking while trying to see what that something is)
took/
the "n" out of a word/& was left with nothing/
but/
"e-g-r-o"/

I/   (Man wearing orange tries to find out, too!)
took/
the "e" out of a word/that left me with just enuf/so that/
I could always be reminded of my not forgotten past/in order/
that/
I don't get trapped into living my present life in vain/
while all the time/making way/for a plentiful tomorrow/

I/   (Man wearing blue)
took the "gee" out of a word/
& found nothing but pieces of a jigsaw puzzle/
that/
needed to be solved/for I was still left holding the bag filled with "r eeeeeee o's"/

I/   (Man wearing purple)
took the "r" out/
then/
the "o" & was left with a most sweet tasty thang!/a double fudge cookieeeeeeeee!!!/
with its most tasty white cream.../

        (Both men run after man wearing purple & his cookies off stage left/lights fade out...)

ACT II...

Movements in time...Man-to-Man Relationships

THEN...(mid-50s to late 80s)

> "In bringing many sons to glory it was fitting that God, for whom and through whom everything exists, should make the author of their salvation perfect through suffering." (**Hebrews 2:10**)

( )   (Enters entire cast gathers on stage)

THEN...

I

Bessie Smith/   (Man wearing black)
in the early 30s/warned me about makin'...makin' love/
...makin' love...love in the dark/

now/as things start to come to light/
I/
attempt to hide my shame/content with groping through life seeking you/

Billie Holiday/   (Man wearing orange)
later/pulled my coat tail...warning me/
about staying away from those strange fruit t-r-e-e-sssssssss/
saying/
prevention is a lot safer/
than/
losing one's soul.../

Lady Day/
sometimes happy/sometimes blu'/
but/
like her/we must all someday pay some heavy dues.../
just to make it to the next day/

then/   (Man wearing white)
Mahalia Jackson/
lifted/my low-life & broken down spirits/
by/cleansing my soul/as I sometimes/prayed/she was singing, "Precious Lord"/
just for me/

yes/
indeed take my hand/
I/am blind/but/hope someday/that/that I might truly see what's right now in
front/
& tomorrow/maybe/a head of me/

Lil Richard/   (Man wearing beige speaks whiling pulling out a makeup kit)
long before Dionne Warwick/
showed me/what amazin' things one can do/with a little make-up & hairdo…

Mr. Chuck Berry/   (Man wearing purple)
taught me how to roll around/
with a gal named Lucille/& even Elvis rocked me/until…/
until I heard something/about/Negroes & his blue suede shoes, umh?/

Oh, no…/   (Man wearing red)
not the stepping on them part/
it was…/it was…/was something about/yeah…/shining shoes & nig…

but/   (Man wearing black cuts off man wearing red,
the/   right before he get's the "N" word out!)
King is dead!/long live the King…/
besides, according to LOOK or was it LIFE magazine…/
Elvis/
never owned a pair of blue suede shoe…/
But Big Mama Thornton/
sang, "You ain't nothing but a hound dog…"/
& Elvis/opted to hide out in Gracie Mansion/
with pills, women & booze…/
now /
about the nig…/   (Man wearing black is cut off by the man wearing red again)

see/   (Man wearing beige cuts off men wearing black & looking at man wearing red)
i've/
learned/lately in my young adult life/
that/
if/someone is likely/to talk about someone else/you can be damn sure/
that/the next time/
they'll be talking about you!   (Man wearing beige looking
                                at man wearing red & audience)

yeah/   (Man wearing white)
Mr. Berry & Lil Richard/
& good golly Ms. Molly, Lucille & Elvis, Lady Day/
& good ole Bessie Smith/they/all/held me spellbound…perhaps it was…/

yeah! perhaps it was/   (Man wearing black speaks cutting off man wearing white)
to much of Ms. Molly/

& to much of Lucille/from the night before.../
seeing/as we all bounced right in the 60s without skipping a beat/
unprepared/for yet another one of life's battles.../
the Civil Rights Era & Kennedy Mania/

II

(Man wearing blue...woman enters & sit down at table drinking)

Lil Stevie Wonder/
damn near/
made me want to adopt him/
when he asked: "If you really love me..."/
as I sat/& watched mama sip from another fifth of Gordon's Gin/
all because/Papa had decided to join the Rolling Stones.../
only/to roll as far as/to the house next door/
over & over/again & again.../

I've listened to mama/   (Man wearing orange)
playing/
Aretha's "Don't play that song for me..."/

(Man wearing beige starts to sing the lyric only...)

over & over/
again & again "cause it only brings back memories..."/

mama's pain/
I didn't understand, "I was only seventeen, I didn't think you be so mean..."/

mama/   (Man wearing red, while looking a man wearing beige as if he's crazy)
had been beaten/
down/with so many lies/
that
fighting back with the truth/was just to much for her/

then/   (Man wearing beige, cutting off man wearing red...)
the girls of Motown/
Berry Gordy's dream girls/
cried out for my Papa, too "Stop in the name of love..."/
but/
Papa only came back.../only to leave again/

(32)   BlAcKpOeMoLoGy

this/
time for good/carryin' his bags/& all of his medals from Korea/
mama/said nothing/while her sisters called her a got damn fool/

for mama/   (Man wearing black, looking over at the woman...)
that was the last straw.../
she screamed/she cried & moan & damn near burned/
the whole got damn house down/
mama/
stop going/to the market/
she/
stop counting her toes/& choosed to stay home/
while continuing to sip her Gordon's Gin/

my po' mama/   (Man wearing brown speaks/while walking
is now/   toward the woman who dies in his arms)
holding on to the hem of God almighty's garment/
listening to Mahalia singing: "Soon be done trouble of the world..."/

            (Man wearing beige starts to humming this song...to a soft fade)

the angel's/   (Man wearing black)
had carried mama/
home,/with a chorus of..."Gotta find me an angel...to fly away w/me..."/

& "Amazing grace..."/   (A quartet starts to sing this song...to a soft fade.)
mama's favorite gospel song/
which I now play/over & over/again, again...wonderin'/
if/
mama had died from a broken heart/
or/to much of Gordon's Gin?/

then brother James Brown/   (Man wearing green)
begged/
the entire world to: "Please, Please, Please, don't go..."/
but/it didn't stop.../it didn't stop me from going off to fight in the Vietnam War/

while America/   (Man wearing black)
sat & watched/watched & sat/
as/my brothers & sisters tore up/their/very own homes/shops & streets/
all cross/
Haarlem/Chicago/Watts/while schools of black Panthers & common folk alike.../

became outraged/because the real King.../& Malcolm/was shot down like dogs/
by dogs/its funny.../mad in fact/I'm off fightin'/to make this country free/
& some of my people/have decided/
that/it's better to steal a TV set instead of guns & razor blades/
like Gil-Scott Heron said: "this revolution shall not be televised..."/
I/   (Man wearing red)
guess they were watchin' to much of the racist/
"I Love Lucy,"/
it's ironic/
how America could have fallen in love with Ricky Ricardo/
& have so much hatred & resentment for Castro/
hell even/Castro convertibles were.../
I/mean were stolen too!!!/

it's funny/   (Man wearing black)
mad in fact/I was off/
fightin' to keep this country free/
& America sat & watched/my brothers & sisters/
screwing on some sofa bed/
stolen/from Woolworth's display windows/not carin'/
if they pissed/off the boss man.../while wonderin'/
if he & his city Klan members.../the Knight's of Columbus ever offered/
a scholarship to the Nostrand Avenue ole Boys High School in Brooklyn, NYC/
or to the NAACP/from the Woolworth's stores.../
God only knows/
that/the Negros in the Bed-Stuy community/
shop there every check day/in those Woolworth stores/
off of Nostrand Avenue & Fulton St./the 1st & 16th/of every month/

on check day?/   (Man wearing purple, as if questioning the significance of the day)

check day?/   (Man wearing green)

check day?/   (Man wearing white)

then/   (Man wearing black)
I returned back from the war/
only to start one of my very own/

you/   (Man wearing red)
see I couldn't relate.../
I couldn't relate & I wasn't relating.../

(34)   BlAcKpOeMoLoGy

to black women/
mama was gone.../
& maybe/I've been away to long?/

&/   (Man wearing black)
no matter/how hard I had tried to leave/
the demons between the legs of Ms. Kim's in Vietnam/
they/had all followed me back to America...this sweet land of liberty.../

maybe/   (Man wearing red)
i've been away/
been away to long.../

yeah/   (Man wearing beige)
maybe?/

the 70s/   (Man wearing red)
had done turned/
my brothers & my sisters/into Hollywood tough guys/
pimps & whores/with names/like Superfly & Sheba baby.../

whatever happen to names like Leroy Jones & Esther Mae/
or better yet *Kwesi* (Kway-see) & *Binta* (Been-tah)/
Nigeria names/
meaning *conquering* & *close to my heart*/
or/
West afrikan names like/
Tuere (Too-air-ray) meaning *sacred*/
or/
Camara (Kah-mah-rah) meaning *teacher*.../

upon/   (Man wearing yellow)
seein'/
that/
I was no longer a child or adolescent of the 30s, 40s, 50s nor 60s/
but/
a man of the 70s/
I looked for a sister.../a sister like/Diahann Carroll.../
for she was/
the only positive black image/that I could remember/of one together sister/
but/
I still couldn't relate to black women.../

maybe/   (Man wearing red)
yeah, maybe/
i've been away/
to long/
I have been away/   (Man wearing brown)

I have been away/   (Man wearing green)

I have been away/   (Man wearing yellow)

to long/   (Man wearing black)
off fightin' some got damn war/
that/
has now imprisoned me/

now/   (Man wearing red)
i'm hooked/
hooked on a...a white thang/a white & beautiful thang/
the perfect lady & I shall call her smack/

while/   (Man wearing brown)
my new found/
lady & I were strung out on some/American street corner/
we heard/Marvin Gaye & the Temptations singin'/
(while we were) flyin' high on "cloud no. 9"/
asking a question: "What' going on...what's happen' brother?"/

          (Man wearing brown is looking at man wearing red who is nodding off...)

as/   (Man wearing white)
I/
searched the blue skies & white clouds/
for mama...for mama to give me an answer/
& mama did/
for you see.../
even a mother's love...even a mother's love is alive in the spirit.../
which forced me back into a state of reality/

for/   (Man wearing black)
I was near/my very own death/or going crazy/
which is basically the same damn thing/

upon hearing/   *(Man wearing orange)*
the maddening/screams/of soldiers shooting/
at the Vietnamese innocent children/

upon hearin'/   *(Man wearing green)*
the cries of my mama'/broken heart/

upon hearin'/   *(Man wearing purple)*
the cries from/my very own mouth/
the nightmares/the sleepless night.../the angry mornings.../the bitter days.../

cries/   *(Man wearing beige)*
of dyin' people/ listenin' to death/
while stealin' from the livin'/
then/
again/perhaps a combo of both!/

dyin'/   *(Man wearing black)*
& goin' crazy/at the same time/

then/   *(Man wearing blue)*
brother Marvin Gaye/
pulled me up/from out of the gutter/
removin' the noose from around my neck/
saying: over & over/again & again/you're lookin' for "trouble man"/

        (Looking over at the man wearing red, who is still nodding...)

nothin'/but trouble, as I forgot it was brother man Gaye.../
& not Brother Isaac Hayes who was the troubled man.../

then/   *(Man wearing black walks toward the woman/*
Bro. Issac Hayes/   *who has transformed into another woman)*
introduced/me to a sister named Roberta Flack/
who helped "...*bridge me over some trouble waters*"/

then/   *(Man wearing white speaks while the music is played softly in the background)*
stroked me softly/
with her song/called: "*Ballad of the Sad young men...*"/
in "*Trying times like these...*" & "*...killing me softly.*"/
while/
Isaac Hayes made me feel things were more secured in loving a fine sister again/

by lifting off/that ugly white thang called smack/

unlockin'/   (Man wearing black)
my mental chains/
& allowin' me to "Stand Accused..."/
of lovin' smack,/booze & the blues/& white women, too!/

realizing/   (Man wearing yellow)
that a mind,/a mind is a terrible thing/
to screw up.../over something/that one/should/
consider a total/waste of time/

brother Barry white/   (Man wearing brown)
taught me/
the magical/
musical words: "Baby, oooooooo baby!" & I now know the true meaning.../

...behind/   (Man wearing orange, while taking the woman from the other man)
the blacker the berry/
the sweeter the juice/baby/for i'm now in love with a love unlimited/oh! baby, oooooooooo!/

        (Man wearing brown speaks, while attempting to step toward the woman/who exits)

yeah/
a sister all my own!/

then/   (Man wearing beige)
Diana Ross/
woke me up/with a serious, "Love Hangover".../
probably from loving herself to much/
then/
again not really/cause it pays to be ones own boss!!!/

then/   (Man wearing purple)
came Gloria Gaynor,/
who found out & responded back.../
to all black men: "I will survive..." U "...double-crossing two timing..." SOB/

just/   (Man wearing beige)
because she wasn't my First Choice.../

& just/   (Man wearing black)
when I was/
startin' to relate to black women.../

now/   (Man wearing red, as he tries to compose himself)
I have to fight them off/
something/
society calls: a black male shortage/
due to black-on-black crime/being in prison, or one being gay?/

                    Man wearn red once again looks over at man wearing beige)

you/   (Man wearing beige is ignoring man wearing red)
see/
Donna Summer's/
introduced me to some Village People/
who told me about having some fun at the "YMCA"/
yeah/maybe? Donna.../
then/
she left me alone/only to be/swept across the disco dance floors/
with/
black & white men in tight Calvin Klein jeans/
waving/bamboo fans.../usin' tambourines better than/
the NJ Mass Choir/expressin' themselves/blowin' whistles/
& screamin' *"get it girl..."*/to Ms. Donna Summer's/
as she continued to bake her cake in MacArthur's Park/while cryin'
in the rain/with Barbara Steisand/'cause she had to settle for the crumbs/
it's hard tryin'/to get over singin' *"enuf is enuf..."*/

when/   (Man wearing black)
all i ever wanted was to just get in.../

I then told the Jones Girls/   (Man wearing blue)
they/
were going to make me *"Love Somebody Else"*/
while all the time I was thinking real hard about joining the YMCA/

yeah/   (Man wearing orange)
then/
they/responded back with:

              (Woman speaks this from off stage...then reappears centers stage)

                   "...there will never be peace in this world,
                     until man is at peace with his woman."

which is something to think about?/   *(Man wearing black)*
think about?/   *(Man wearing red)*

think about?/   *(All the men in unison)*

as/   *(Man wearing beige speaks while looking around the stage)*
the Jones Girls/
caught me (& some of you)/paying our membership dues in order to join the
YMCA/

brother's/   *(Man wearing white)*
had better wake up!/
see the 80s have come & gone/
& Christianity has swept up Donna Summer/
placin' a protective hedge around her/
but/
who's going to sweep up & protect you, my brother'.../
like/Sylvester said from: *"feeling mighty real..."*/

see A.I.D.S./   *(Man wearing black)*
is here/
& if it's left up to some power'/
that be/it'll be here to stay/

there was/   *(Man wearing brown)*
a time/
when sisters Tramaine Hawkins & the Clark Sisters/
had taken over the dance floors/
perhaps/
Donna Summer' you should have stayed a disco diva/
for/those/girls were preachin' to all of God's children.../
preachin' of God's grace & mercy/

with songs like/   *(Man wearing beige)*
"fall down on me..."/
& *"you bring me peace..."*/
& *"joy in the morning time..."*/
& *"you made my day..."*/

now it's brother Kirk Franklin & the Family with *"Stomp"*/
in their attempt to bring the Generation X to Christ/

what if:/   (Man wearing purple)
sister Tina Turner/
done told the entire world that she's looking out for #1/
& to hell with all black men/(who wouldn't after Ike?)/
& Christianity, too!/

she's now singin' "What's love got to do...got to do...got to do?"/
& chanting NAM-yo-RENGO-kyo/
& I finally thought.../I had found some peace/
when/
I found/a Nubian sister like you?/

now/   (Man wearing black)
i'm an old man.../
having been in & out of love/
& always in some state of conflict or battle/with no peace left to be found/

then/   (Man wearing orange)
here comes/
Whitney, Sister Tata Vega & CeCe & BeBe/
hey, "Maybe God is trying to tell me something?"/
they/
were telling me "...to hold up the light"/
from/
the darkness of Bessie's singing the blues/
to/
a white boy named George Michael's/singing about one "needing to have a little faith..."/

4 I had found out/   (Man wearing black)
U-2 my beautiful nubian sister/
"haven't found out what you've been looking for..."/
as you walked/out of my door.../

yeah/   (Man wearing red)
now, that Ms. Jackson/
& yes i'm being "Nasty"/
now/
that she has told you about being in "Control"/
you/
opted to just leave me...woman...have you done lost your mind?/

leaving me/   *(All the men say this to the woman except the man wearing beige)*
uhm?/
& walking out of my door!/

yeah/   *(Man wearing red)*
done packed up/
& skip town/
& i'm thinking perhaps I shall see you again?/

leaving me!/   *(Man wearing black)*
the nerve!/
yeah, but we shall met again.../
for Ms. Jackson told me, too! *"That's the way love goes."*/

as/   *(Man wearing beige)*
we all prepare for your new beau's/
the artist formerly known as Prince party/
to end all parties in the year..."1999"/
than/
there's/all of these new kids on the block.../
from Lil Kim to Puffy Daddy,...
(&/or Bebe Winans going sole singing "Thank You"...at Gay Clubs...
once again, bring God to the children, who don't go to church...")or/
the remaking...and/or the sampling of songs/
songs that tells my entire life story/
& now that Ms. Janet's *"Together Again,"*/
but *"Where have all the flowers gone..."* Ms. Janet?/
...you're just a little to late, Ms. Thang!/

but i'll/   *(Man wearing red, cutting of man wearing beige)*
be an old man come "1999"/
but/
i'll still ask you for a slow dance/
because/beautiful black woman.../

yeah/   *(Man wearing black...hands the woman some flowers)*
I'm/
still.../so much in love with you/
& hey you can't tell me/there's nothing like an old fool!!!/

(Lights fade out, only the woman exits...carry off flowers...)

(   )

(All the men are on stage in a setting which resembles any city neighborhood...
a screen drops down, projecting images of a city playground, park and streets.)

I

I did not realize the love/   (Man wearing beige)
until there were none/

I did not realize the fun/   (Man wearing orange)
until I felt I had none/

I did not remember the laughter/   (Man wearing purple)
until I watched the other children/
in the vicinity of my several Brooklyn streets.../

other children/   (Man wearing black)
who were calling out for their daddies/
& I recall having none to call out too.../

II

I recall undressing in locker rooms/   (Man wearing beige)
feeling inadequate & blameworthy.../
cursing all the God's/while thinking that perhaps I should have been born a girl.../
instead of a boy/

until/   (Man wearing black)
I learned/
that much later in life...big things...do come in small packages.../

yet/   (Man wearing red looks at man wearing beige)
penis envy/
can be a bitch at times.../

III

I remember always being heart broken/   (Man wearing beige)
always being heart broken/& broken hearted/

over never having been picked for anyone's: baseball, football, basketball teams.../
until/I found out/
that/
havin' muscles & patting each other on the ass/don't make a man...a man!/

(Looking back at the man wearing red...)

only love of self/   (Man wearing green)
through loving other'/was I able to cross/
this/dark passage into early manhood/

now/   (Man wearing purple)
with these memories/memories of a confused/
& disenchanted childhood/not to mention/those banal/teen years.../

somehow/   (Man wearing white)
causin' the term paternalism & me to feel nothin'/
nothin' but pure contentions.../contention-ness toward/
what may have now/been called: "those growing adulthood years..."

IV

I/   (Man wearing beige)
do recall the love.../the love unspoken/
but/
love nevertheless/

the/   (Man wearing green)
love that I had.../I had found/
came from a man God saw fit to call home/call home at an early age/

leaving me/   (Man wearing orange)
in his watchful eye/& like the denied stone/
I/
have learned to stand alone in the mist of life stormy battles/

because/   (Man wearing beige)
I do believe that my father/
by the grace of God/is watching over me/

I/   (Man wearing red)
do remember/

the comics books/& playboy magazines/
that...I often read after he did...just before going off to bed.../

I/   (Man wearing yellow)
often laugh a lot/every now & then/
over the bitter sense-less-ness/
the tears/the fears/& oh, those wasted years/

the years I have spent/   (Man wearing beige)
dwelling in sorrowful memories.../
memories of my very own/

God/   (Man wearing brown)
has truly blessed me/
blessed me with this opportunity of forgiveness/

&/   (Man wearing blue)
as I continue to dwell in my father's house/
a house with rooms/that only a mansion could hold/

for I am now/   (Man wearing black)
a father to others/
& now havin' watch my children playing off in a nearby parks/
& having a son/
& in unison having the both of us say.../
Daddy/we (I)/love you in our very own special way.../

        (Each man embraces one another, except the men wearing red & beige)

(   )

fatherhood/   (Man wearing black starts talking to all the men...)
don't play it cheap, fellas!/
it's a hefty price for one to pay/even if it isn't for keeps/
for in later years/father-hood/has to share/it's rightful place/
among the roles of:
husband-hood/work-hood/friendship-hood/
personal-hood & community-hood/

last/
but/
far from least...manhood!/

I could've walk away…leaving me, myself & I all alone/
with/what some may have called selfish-hood/
yes/
fatherhood/don't play it cheap, fellas!/nor take it for granted/
for/it is a costly investment/
but/
the high hopes of the out come/
& benefits…my brother/
the hugs/& numerous innocent kisses in the end is the sky the limit'…/

(All the men start to exit, except for the man wearing green…)

(   )

you may ask, why?…why?/   (Man wearing green)
my brother, well for example:

the broken television set/
the soggy cereal/the soiled/
soaked blankets/& the empty band-aid case/
& the broken Christmas toys (that, I'm still paying for)/
& all the why not's/
& all of the how comes…daddy?/
& all the I don't knows…daddy?/

please take my kids…will you?/   (Man wearing green is now
then again/   addressin' the audience)
on a second note/i'll think…/i'll keep them/
just a little longer/to give them hell…/
for you see/in my second childhood/some called ole age/
or better yet/
senile dementia…/   (Man wearing green exit, while lights fade)

(   )

(Enters man wearing beige speaking…with man wearing red standing off up stage left.)

I must confess/
that/
fairies & their tales are true/true & should be respected/
all fairies tales/whether told as black princes'
running through the deep congos of Africa/or/

riding the "el" trains in the south Bronx of NYC/
tales of these black princes getting off.../
getting off near the Grand Concourse/
with anyone who dares to show them just a lil affection/
of course/men & others like them/all have one thing in common/
they all think with their respective heads/
that's/
why/
there's always a love & hate relationship/   (Looking over at man wearing red)
cause they end up producing/
lil boys/
like/
androgyny & me.../

        (Man wearing beige exits giggling stage right/
  while pretending he's applying lipstick...then the lights goes down on man wearing red)

(   )

        (A flash of light and then the enter cast emerges...)

first day of class/   (Man wearing black)
all the men/sat on one side of the room/
while all the women sat on the other side

the women/   (Woman enters...man wearing white speaks...)
entered/by groups of:

one, two, three at a time/

the men/   (Man wearing black speaks...All the men move about in a single file...)
came in single file/
already knowin' their place/

the outline for the day's course/   (Man wearing white)
was to study humans & their relationships w/one another/

but/   (Man wearing black)
the women/
started talkin' & asking question'/

the men/   (Man wearing white)
just sat there/knowin' their place, again!/

during recess/   (Men wearing black & white in unison)
the women/talked about last night' miniseries/

(Woman speaks all female parts)

"oh, girl...when that woman's baby die
from stickin' that fork into
that electrical outlet..."

"I know honey/I went around the entire house
plugging up every hole I could fine...including my very own."

"Yeah, my child left a toy soldier in the refrigerator the other night...
right near the Welch's grape jelly/
I figured someone like me ought to know
what it's like to be left standin' out in the cold,
so I left the soldier there, too!"

(Man wearing black & white in unison...All the other men are group in a single file...)

the men just sat there/
knowing their place once again.../   (Men wearing black & white in unison)

"Girl, I know what you mean...
the other day, I was in the shower...
I had placed his & mine...i mean our child on the potty
then after the child had done...
done his business,
the child & I opted for a bath instead
& said, Mr. Bubbles, oh, please take us awaaaaaay!!!"

"...how old is yours"

"Girl...14 months...and the other one is 6 years old..."

"mine are too...I have a 2 & 3 years old child"

the men/   (Man wearing black & white in unison)
just sat there/knowing their place/
once again/

"...you haven't see anything yet...just wait...it get's worst,
before it gets better...child!"

after recess/   *(Man wearing white)*
the entire class was called.../back into session/

the men/   *(Man wearing black)*
were all in their places/
yet/ease droppin'/

ease droppin'/   *(Man wearing white)*
on the women/women talkin' about humans & their relations/
while at the same time/the men/just sat there.../

> *(Man wearing black...all the men gather up there belongings & in a single file they exits right behind the woman/The men wearing purple, green, blue and orange and brown enters)*

feelin' left out in the cold.../   *(Man wearing black)*

(This poem can be omitted for brevity...)

I

it's always at night/   *(Man wearing orange)*
when images of dancing tongues/will often appear/
brushing against the nape of someone's forgotton son.../

some mothers/   *(Man wearing blue)*
may watch their children/
fall/
as they attempt to stand & walk alone/
but/
that same mother/may remain content to just watching/
their child crawl & every now/
& then/wipe/that child off & send them off to play/

yet/   *(Man wearing purple)*
when a man falls.../

a woman in love/   *(Woman enters and embraces man wearing purple)*
can only embrace him/
in her tender arms/bath him with warm tears/while he pounces & pounces/
upon the center of her total being/
while/he attempts to keep from/crying/
like mama's lil boy...   *(Woman exit)*

a father/   (Man wearing green)
maybe proud to hear the words:

"I'm having your child..."/   (Woman speaks...from off stage)

& eagerly awaits the arrival/
of his God sent child/praying that life will be a little tender & kindlier/
with his or hers feelings/
& maybe that child will someday turn into something other/
than lil boy blu'/

papa/may have/   (Man wearing brown)
mama/may have/
yet/
God truly blesses the child that may well have his own/
while standing alone.../

sis'/   (Man wearing blue)
heard of the rumors/
told about lil boy blu'/
then reached for the elmer's glue/in her attempts in trying to put together/
another black brother...fucked up life' jigsaw puzzle/
only to get beaten down/herself.../by finding out too, just a little to late/
with a man of her very own/

young brothers/   (Man wearing green)
may rub elbows amongst themselves/
in their dark bedrooms/under tented firmly erected cum stained sheets/

then/   (Man wearing purple)
grow up into manhood/feeling guilty & down/
right sinful/
that/
they often/resent being a man/standing all alone.../unless scoring a touchdown

then/   (Man wearing orange)
goes/
the brotherly love.../as lil boy blu' & the wide end receivers/
pats each other on their padded asses.../

II

...&/   (Man wearing blue)
friends may support/your every deed/good or even bad/
but behind closed doors/laugh behind your back.../
calling you the fool/

but/   (Man wearing orange)
remember/lil boy blu'/
that/true friends/never/put one another to a test/
after learnin'/
this for ones self.../one can truly stand alone

lil boy blu'.../   (Man wearing green)
have faith in everyone/especially yourself...

mother/   (Man wearing blue)
father/
sister/
brother/
& friends alike/

&/   (Man wearing orange)
most certainly in the spirit of the God within...Amen!/

as/   (Man wearing purple)
you crawl about this world/
while/coming in from being left out in the cold/
&/becoming a much better man for having done so/
by/
standing/erect/strong & on your very own.../

(Exits men wearing purple, green, orange & brown. Remaining is man wearing blue,
who is joined by both men wearing red & white)

(   )

a dream on hold/   (Man wearing blue)
I/
have/

a dream on hold/   (Man wearing red)

I/
have/

a dream on hold/   (Man wearing white)
I/
have/
that only/
I/
can see/

I/
have a dream on hold/
that/
stretches far beyond the mightiest of seas/

that/   (Man wearing blue leaps into mid-air)
can fly higher than a soaring eagle/

that/   (Man wearing red)
has lasted longer then a Broadway show/

that's/   (Man wearing white…in the voice of Dr. Martin Luther King, Jr.)
taller/
then a mountain top/

a dream on hold/   (Man wearing blue)
I/
have/
yes/a dream on hold/
I/
have/

but/   (Man wearing red)
for/
right now/I will keep it between/just/me & the good Lord above…/

(   )

(Lights fade out…then rises again, we see the woman entering stage left & she
sits center stage; where a chair has been placed. We can see she is with child.
Men wearing red, white & blue are joined by the other men throughout this monologue.
Enters man wearing black is holding a box of corn starch and hands it to the woman.)

with no arms to rest your weary head upon/
& with no shoulder for you to lean on/
& with no mail comin' today to bring you no bad news, mama/

news from welfare/   (Man wearing blue)

news from your man/   (Enters man wearing brown)

news from Ed McMahon/   (Enters man wearing beige)

nor the fucking pony express/   (Man wearing red)

(Man wearing black speaks, while all the other men continues to enter
& circle around the woman who is looking for another chair)

with bills piling up/you've done seen the rabbit die.../since last month's rent was
due/
& your man is gone, now/

no placing one' feet.../   (Man wearing beige)
placing one' feet/in shining new bronze booties

(Man wearing green speaks, while holding up a empty frame in one hand & a picture in the other)

no pictures of white models in cardboard picture frames.../

see nothing fits!/   (Man wearing red...referring to the white models)

causin' your unborn to being/   (Man wearing brown)
label another child born/
without a silver spoon in his or her mouth/

I/   (Man wearing black)
know...mama/

(Man wearing green brings another chair out and places it center stage)

I/
know/
that/
you're in need of a chair/a chair with a strong back mama/
yet/
you're in need of a chair/yes mama/you're in need of a chair.../
a chair/with a strong sturdy back/

I/
see/
that/the old chair had done gave out, mama/

see nothing seems to fit!/   (Man wearing red)

your man.../   (Man wearing green)

nothing seems to fit.../   (Man wearing red)

your family.../   (Man wearing green)

nothing seems to fit.../   (Man wearing red)

your welfare case.../   (Man wearing green)

see nothing seems to fit!/   (Man wearing red)

nothing!!!/   (Both men in unison)

no support/   (Man wearing black)
no support for the load/
for the load/you can't/but must carry alone, mama/

nor did anyone else/   (Man wearing red)
offer you support.../you thought they would/
yet no one could/would/or felt they should.../felt they should, mama.../
help you carry such/a heavy burden.../

I/   (Man wearing black)
know, mama.../

you called a friend.../   (Man wearing brown)
called a friend yesterday/
& asked that same friend/to stop by with a softer pillow/
maybe a good book/& a bowl of hot chicken soup/perhaps a warm smile.../

I/   (Man wearing black)
know...mama/

that same friend/   (Man wearing red)
never came...mama/

you mama/   (Man wearing blue)
said:

"I'm the one who's to blame..."   (Woman speaks this part...)

I/   (Man wearing black)
know, mama.../

you're in need of a chair/   (Man wearing green)
a chair with a good strong back/
a chair with a good strong sturdy back/
to ease away the back pains from the load he could not carry.../
just that one night.../

I/   (Man wearing black)
know, mama.../

(All the men start chanting... "I know mama..." as they all move towards
the woman, who's moaning grows louder & louder & turns to soft sobs & a muffled scream...)

I know/   (Man wearing black)
mama.../

mama/
I know.../

(Lights start to dim slowly & the woman is the only one slowly walking off stage/
All the men freezes in their places)

(   )

she was never the type/   (Lights come up on man wearing orange)
yes/
all the odds were against her/

being/   (Man wearing red)
young/gifted & black/

she/   (Man wearing beige)
was a child/having a child/

she/   (Man wearing blue)
was brought up on pot-luck dinners/
& hand-me-downs deserts/

along/   (Man wearing purple)
with seven other nappy headed/
& loveless chillus/

yes/   (Man wearing orange)
she never was the type/

the/   (Man wearing brown)
eldest out of seven/her mama/never paid debts on time
because/there was always another mouth to feed/

then/   (Man wearing beige)
one day/he/came & came/
& came & came again & again.../

she never mentioned/   (Man wearing brown)
havin' no father to teach her right from wrong/

but/   (Man wearing beige)
mama did/the best she could/

mama/   (Man wearing brown)
tried to pick.../
to pick up the young girl' low life spirits/

no preacher.../   (Man wearing beige)
to preach a sermon come early Sunday morning/
& no teacher to pass a red apple of knowledge & understandin' unto her.../

because/   (Man wearing brown)
her very own mama/
never learned life'/golden rules...she didn't either/

seven chillus/   (Man wearing beige)
could have told her/that/

you see/   (Man wearing orange)
she was never/
the type/
being/
young/gifted & black/

(Man wearing beige noticing that the man wearing red is uncomfortable/
he tends to over do it...)

then/one day/he came.../
/& came/
& came/
& came again/
& again/

a complete stranger/   *(Man wearing brown)*
like a thief in the middle of the night/
he came.../

stealing something of hers.../   *(Man wearing beige)*
when he left/he left/leavin' nothing but shame/
& guilt in it's place/

another/   *(Man wearing orange)*
young child'/ spirit was taken away.../

now/   *(Man wearing brown)*
mama' daughter & child number 9/
must make due/without paying mo' debts on time/

& I guess after all/   *(Man wearing black)*
mother & child/
have both learned a valuable lesson in life/
& that' to pass the next stranger right.../
right on by.../

(All the men in unison chants "passes the next stranger right on by," as they all exit. Lights dim out)

(This poem can be omitted for brevity...)

(Enters men wearing white & purple/Man wearing white speaks first)

pretty little thing/so black & blue/tell me is it true?/

have we all learned/   *(Man wearing purple)*
to sing the blues.../
seein' the vintage of ones soul/while embracing the morning blazing sun/causin' a dry/
thirst to engulf a lovely & hungry child/who' innocent yearning & passion for life/
is forever placed on hold.../waiting for one day to drink to ones content/

it may leave/   (Man wearing white)
a taste of nectar & bitter sweetness/
of mama' barin' forbidden fruit in rememberin'/
without really thinking another day is nearin'.../

while you sleep/   (Man wearing purple)
my child/the blues play a lament of sorrows/the evening stars/
dance among your nappy edges/& now that the pages of your life has turned/
& a new chapter has begun/

tiny hot pebbles/   (Man wearing white)
dances a dance of wishful waves/leaving one' soul/
touching the earth' core/as the frantic sounds of a heavy beat/
conveys a message of broken spirits/

among the misty air/   (Man wearing purple)
the message becomes crystal clear/
that another chilly night is near/

it' a must for me/   (Man wearing white)
my child to tell you to get up & brush off the dust.../
for mama' apron string can no longer hold you.../
no mo' silky clothes/will be draped against the canvass of life's bitter pill/
& with a sharp knife you'll stab at the open skies/
watching the clouds bleed sweet spirits.../ sweet spirits of sweet rain.../

windy sounds/   (Man wearing purple)
will carry mama's pretty angel burdens/
down to the earth's ground/

so/   (Man wearing white)
much for feeling so black & blue/
cause living knows no other color/

just listen/   (Both men in unison as well exit stage left...)
to your mama/she'll tell you.../

(   )

(Enters men wearing red, beige & yellow from stage right.
Man wearing yellow speaks. Woman enters and sits off right of stage)

mama/yeah/mama dreamt/she dreamt/faded & bitter/dreams.../
dreams/that/turned into nothing.../
nothing/but/collections of old memories/

you.../   (Man wearing beige)
dreamt militant/dreams/while living in america/

you.../   (Man wearing red)
wrote about/including black men into your militant battles/

you mentioned.../   (Man wearing beige)
mentioned something about/black men/
yes/black men in tight jeans/causing a burning desire/
in you to smile.../

Ms. Giovanni?/   (Man wearing yellow)
when/
speaking of my house.../
were you speaking from experience?/

a/   (Man wearing red)
house is a house/
but/our home...we all know is a long way off/
from this 'weet land of liberty.../

let' not even mention/   (Man wearing beige)
the part about/justice for all/& our forty arces/
& one got damn mule.../

as you bathed/   (Man wearing yellow)
in scented oils/on loan from Queen Nefertiti/
while living in the Congo.../
did Hannibal actually give you Rome for a present?/

mama/   (Man wearing beige)
smiles often as she read/
about you seeking pleasure from a running faucet/

I/   (Man wearing yellow)
later realized/that/mama was/lonely too!/

then/   (Man wearing beige)
there was the neighborhood kid.../
a kid named Nikki Rosa/

mama/   (Man wearing red)
use to press Nikki Rosa's nappy lil head/
with her left hand/while reading/your life poetry/
with her right hand/
confirmin'/the ole sayin':

(Spoken by the woman)

"...never let the left hand know...what your right hand is doin'..."

& mama smiled/   (Man wearing beige)
about your passage of black men in tight jeans/
yeah/i've seen mama looking, too!/

but/   (Man wearing red)
you know how some men are.../
daddy/often got lonely, too! & sought after some girl name Sue/

yeah/   (Man wearing yellow)
mama dreamt faded/
& bitter dreams.../dreams/that/turned into nothing/
but collections of broken ole memories/

you.../   (Man wearing beige)
dreamt of militant dreams & black men in tight jeans/

when speaking of my house/   (Man wearing yellow)
Ms. Giovanni/were you speaking from experience?/

yeah!/   (All three men in unison)

I/   (Man wearing red)
remember you.../
you taught me about revolutions & the Vietnam war/
& introduced me to the Rev. James Cleveland/
as we both stood on the banks of Jordan/askin' peace to be still.../

peace/be still.../   (Man wearing yellow) peace be still.../   (Man wearing beige)

yeah/   (Man wearing yellow)
Nikki Rosa & me/
we/had/a lil revolution of our very own/

yeah, in the back staircase/   (Man wearing beige very sarcastically)
of some dirty old haarlem tenement/

while/   (Man wearing red)
mama/moan & smile/
while touching the very spot where Nikki Rosa's head use to rest/
while reading your life poetry/

yeah/   (Man wearing yellow)
mama/
in/her/loneliness/sought/comfort from reading you.../

(All three men exit stage left...with woman slowly following)

(   )

(Enters men wearing orange, blue & brown...man wearing blue starts to speak)

oh! how I long to venture back to the days of my youth/

back to the days/   (Man wearing orange)
when I would toy.../
toy/with the innocent ideas/the innocent hopes/the innocent dreams/that only the
young may have/

dreams now/   (Man wearing blue)
buried at the bottom of my treasured toy chest/

oh!/   (Man wearing brown)
how the days of my youth/
tugs at the back of my mind/leading a clear passage way/
to days long gone bye-bye/

I/   (Man wearing orange)
long to venture/
once again/upon the grassy evergreens of back home/just/one mo' time/

oh!/   (Man wearing blue)
how i'd love/
to kneel down by my mama' side/
while combin' the worries out of her weary head/
as/she rocks off to sleep/just once/just once/just one mo' time/

oh!/   (Man wearing brown)
how I long to venture back to the days of my youth/

but/   (Man wearing orange. Enters woman who starts combing his hair)
this time/
i'll have mama comb out the worries from my weary head/

just once/   (Each man whispers softly, over lapping one another...then they all exits)
just once/
just one mo' time/for a very long, long, long time.../

(   )

            (Enters men wearing purple, white, green & red. Man wearing purple starts to speak)

mama had it all figured out.../
to be/young, gifted & black/was where it was/
& that's.../that!/

yeah/   (Man wearing red)
she/had/it all figured out.../

to be/   (Man wearing green)
in/love at the innocent age of only sweet 16/
meant/giving it all up to Big Jimmy Lee/

yeah/   (Man wearing purple)
mama/didn't figure it all out/
until it was to late/
that/
Big Jimmy Lee/would soon grow tired & skip town for good/

now/   (Man wearing white)
she's/only left with her fade memories/of once being in love/

she/   (Man wearing red)
now/

(62)   BlAcKpOeMoLoGy

dreams of once being young, gifted & black/
& sweet 16…again!/

until/   (Man wearing white)
she grasp at her breast/
& looks down into the eyes of Lil Jimmy Lee, jr./
& his innocence brown eyes/
& pray that her manchild would someday grow up to be some other/
women's joy/
while/that/women/is/also/black, young, gifted/
& sweet 16…/   (They all exit stage right)

(   )

            (Enters men wearing beige, blue & yellow. Man wearing yellow starts to speak)

in the 60s/
both/the/Lawrence Welk & Carol Burnett variety shows
gave me role models/

role models/   (Man wearing beige)
who were black like me:

Arthur Duncan & the brother from the Carol Burnett Show…/
what is that brother's name?/

…men who danced/   (Man wearing blue, cutting off man wearing beige)
in spite of life' many storms/

I told mama…/   (Man wearing yellow)

I told papa…/   (Man wearing blue)

that/   (Man wearing beige)
I had wanted/
to grow up & become just like them/
two black men/who danced/dance & swirl/tap & sway/
just
like my two black heroes…/
the response I got back/
was/the only response/uncultured/mis-educated\mis-represented/
black folks/only/knew back then:

"boy only uncle Tom's & sissy   (Man wearing blue)
want to grow up & dance...
colored folks always want to entertain white folks..."

then/there/was/   (Man wearing beige)
was the notion to take piano lessons/
the same response/once again/from uncultured/mis-educated\mis-represented/
black folks/

so I continued/   (Man wearing yellow)
to watch white Sunday variety shows/

yet/   (Man wearing beige)
only dreaming/of sunny parades/
& pennies from heaven/while my very own kinfolk/
continued to rain on my parade/& bursts my tiny little bubbles/
then/Soul Train came along/& I forgot all about American Bandstand/
yet/as soon as I started to climb aboard/
mama & papa/all of a sudden became uppity Negroes/
challenging me with these words & phrases like...like.../

"...niggers always   (Man wearing yellow)
acting a fool, like they are still in Africa...
doing some nonsense called the robot...turn that television off boy
& go to your room."

or/one of them/   (Man wearing blue)
would get up/& change the channel/searching once again/
for Lawrence Welk & or the Carol Brunett Sunday night variety shows/

I wanted.../   (Man wearing beige)
I needed.../
to search for my blackness & my two role models.../
black men who seemed to love dancin'/

then/   (Man wearing yellow)
I heard about/one black man/

then another/   (Man wearing blue)
who dared to turn their dreams into reality/

then another/   (Man wearing beige)
black man/

(64)   BlAcKpOeMoLoGy

who took drums & colors from Africa & Europe/
& stirred souls with their mixture of jazz/with a touch of America' blues/

healin'/   (Man wearing yellow)
people of colour/through/their music/their art/their dance/
& gift of song in spite of their life' storms/

mama & papa/   (Man wearing beige)
never told me about:

Mr. Arthur Mitchell's Dance Theatre of Harlem/
or/
Mr. Alvin Ailey's dancing at City Center/
or/
Mr. Geoffrey Holder's bringing Timbuktu all the way to Broadway/
nor about the Duke, the Count/
& a some cats name Strayhorn & Miles/

I had to find/   (Man wearing blue)
this all out/from the city streets/
while playing stick-up-kid & drug dealer/

now i'm serving time/   (Man wearing beige)
in a state prison/only dreaming of becomin'/
a real-life artist, one day!/

mama & papa/   (Man wearing yellow)
wrote/
me just the other day/telling me about.../
some kid name Jackson/   (Man wearing beige)
who/dances so BAAAAAD.../

& some brother name Prince/   (Man wearing blue)
who's singin' about some Purple Rain.../

some brother name Lionel/   (Man wearing yellow)
who was dancin' on ceilin'/& singing about:

"Father, watch our children...don't let them fall...cause Jesus is loved..."

& some brother name Wonder/   (Man wearing blue)
who sang about, "Ribbons in the Sky"/

& something/   (Man wearing beige)
called MTV/
where ones gender & color makes no difference/as long/
as one has the talent to Rap/Breakdance/Dirty Dance & Bump & Grind/
themselves all the way to the bank.../

see/   (Man wearing yellow)
that's the trouble/
with some black folks/always the last to know/
what's been dancin' around them.../in their very own backyards/

it's now lock.../   (Enters man wearing black speaking)
lock...lock...& down time/
(Lights out...)

hey/maybe I'll dance now for my parents when I get out.../   (Man wearing beige)

                    (Soft music plays. Men wearing beige, blue & yellow start dancing alone
                       and together to fading lights. Men wearing blue & yellow dances of stage...
                                    men wearing black & beige remain.)

(   )

                    (Man wearing black speaking to man wearing beige...who continues dancing alone)

Hold on to your dreams/for dreams never die/hold on to your dreams/
even if they just up & walks away/
hold on...my brother.../hold on...my brother.../hold on.../
& remember this/by you holding on, it may lead someone new/
to perhaps come your way/hold on to your laughter, 'cause tears don't last forever/
brother learn to laugh at yourself, its a good thing to do.../
Oh! yes, oh yes/for in trying times such as these/when others laugh at you/
for holding on to your dreams/that/they say will surely die/

hold on...my brother.../hold on...my brother.../hold on.../

hold on for dreams never die/& just stand still & know/then/fall back off to sleep.../

                    (Both men wearing black & beige exit embracin' one another.../
                       The woman walks off in total disbelief/while man wearing beige starts to cry)

(   )

(Enter men wearing green, blue & red/while the woman stands off
in the distant/Man wearing green starts to speak)

life seems so hard that I/
on a number of occasions/thought of just giving up/
as I am sure the both of you had felt about giving up on me!/

like the time.../   (Man wearing blue)
I swallowed some Clorox/while hiding/
under the kitchen sink/

mama you blamed daddy/   (Man wearing red...while woman enters sweepin' the floor)
'cause/
he was fixing the plumbing/

daddy you blamed mama/   (Man wearing green takes on the role of the father...)
cause it was her wedding band/
that caused the son-of-a-bitch/sink to clogged up/

mama cried all night long.../
'til this day/no one knows whether she cried/
'cause she thought her ring was lost forever/or/because you called her son.../
a son-of-a-bitch!/but the bottom line/was/that I drank some bleach.../
while hiding under the kitchen sink.../which no one questioned!/

mama' baby.../   (Man wearing blue)
& daddy your manchild/
doctors had declared me for dead/but God step in/& mama & daddy/
you/stop blaming each other/& was thankful for all that you had.../including
me/
remember the time? Mama/   (Man wearing green)
I stole papa' gun/which was fully loaded/
& took it with me to school/intending to pump the principal full of lead/
cause he touched me/the way papa/sometimes touches you/
you & papa lost a days pay/from havin' to visit the principal/& later/
told me about/the birds & the bees/& something to the effect/
that some people are like the birds & birds/& bees & bees/
& that we shall pray for the principal & everyone else like him!/

yes, God step in once again/   (Man wearing blue)
&/you & papa continued to press on/

then came the time.../   (Man wearing green)
the gang & I smoked/
& sold drugs in the school parking lot/
the police/the courts/& even a few nights in jail/shall I go on?/

yeah/   (Man wearing blue)
mama & papa/today/
I thought of giving up...committing suicide.../
but/
God step in once again...& I realize thru God's grace & mercy/
I thank God for parents like you.../
who never gave up on me.../   (They all exit after embracing one another...)

(   )

I/   (Enters men wearing beige, purple, white & orange
stood/   Man wearing beige starts to speak)
on the banks of life grandest runways/

looking for a hero.../   (Man wearing orange)

looking/   (Man wearing purple)
for someone to praise/
& to scold me if redeemed/

like I said looking for a hero/   (Man wearing orange)

for/   (Man wearing purple)
a while/mama was my hero/
cause she was a strong & determined/hard working black women.../
she/at that time was my only choice.../
then/   (Man wearing white)
there was the television/
& all its white images/from/
Superman right on down to Mr. Rogers & Capt. Kangaroo/
nothing positive.../projected in my very own image/but/that was alright.../

for a while.../   (All four men say in unison...)

for a while.../   (Man wearing beige)
I thought of following/
in the footsteps of the neighborhood drag queen/

yeah, I admit flip Wilson'/'Geraldine was on the television/
way before their was RuPaul/then/I found out all that glitter ain't gold/
U see American/has trouble separating fantasy from reality/

see/
what happen/when Wilson teamed up with Gladys's Knight/
without her Pips...(on the short lived sitcom "Charlie & Company")
like I said/
some American's/have trouble.../it's a good thing Bill Cosby came along/
with a positive image/when he did/
'cause...child, these damn heels were killing me...

(Man wearing beige starts looking for his high heels...from before)

for a while.../   (All four men say in unison...again)

the drug dealer'/   (Man wearing purple)
seemed/to have made an impression on me/

the number runner'/   (Man wearing orange)
did too!/then I wanted to don on/
my black power image.../
until a brother stab me in the back/not to mention the many sister'/
who tried to castrate me/cutting me down to a smaller image/
of what they wanted/a black man to be.../
i guess from watching/to much of "One Life To Live"/
rather than finding a real life of their very own.../

for a while.../   (Man wearing purple)
looking for a hero/that/
I had seen in everyone else' father/
but/never in my own/
like I said/   (Man wearing orange)
before.../

I stood on the banks/   (Man wearing beige)
of life' grandest runaway/
waiting to cash in on my father'/father'/father.../
greatest investment.../an investment of reclaiming/
the heir of a black prince/
my/hero/once again.../   (They all run off stage except for the man wearing orange...)

(This poem can be omitted for brevity...)

(Enters men in white & black...man wearing white starts to speak.)

i'll like to write your life poetry/then/have the entire world/
read about it in the mornin's paper/

i'll like to write your life poetry/ (Man wearing black)
while nibbling on your burnt toast/

I want to comb your hair/ (Man wearing white)
while/conversin' with you in your mama' kitchen/
all the wonders of your life poetry/

while/ (Man wearing black)
traveling the subway/
through the city streets/rough & tough/
yet forever on the run/

I could sing a chorus/ (Man wearing white)
from "...every things coming up roses."/
but/I can only afford to give you daisy/

will/you accept them?/ (Man wearing orange)

maybe/maybe not?/ (Man wearing black)

yet/I still would like to write your life poetry.../ (Lights go out...men exit)

(This poem can be omitted for brevity...)

I can't sleep/ (Lights come up...man wearing blue is sitting at a small table
I can't eat/ pouring himself a cup of coffee)
all I do/
is drink/sip & bath my soul in black coffee/all my lonely hours are spent/
with Mr. Coffee & to tell you the truth...W-o-m-a-n!!!/
it doesn't talk back.../talk back...like you!/

I sit here/stirring my life sorrows into an ivory cup/
while/this romance is slowly fading.../by the second/

(Man wearing beige, and all of the remaining men voices are heard from off stage
slowly they all appear in individual spotlights)

by the minute.../   (Man wearing red)

by the hour.../   (Man wearing black)

by the day.../   (Man wearing green)

by the week.../   (Man wearing purple)

by the month.../   (Man wearing white)

by the year.../   (Man wearing orange)

it/   (Man wearing blue looks as if he's hearing voices or going mad)
looks/
as...it looks as...looks...as.../ if it's ending...this romance of ours.../
as...I'd become mo' & mo use to quiet moments/
sitting here drinking with Mr. Coffee/
which remind me of silent moments with you.../   (Lights fade out as the
                                                        man wearing blue exits)

(   )

it was early Saturday morning/   (Man wearing black speaks these words in the dark)
the sun was shining through/
my window & your room for me was still dark!/

                (Lights slowly come up on man wearing black/
            He picks up a brand new cup & pours himself a fresh cup of coffee...)

the breeze parted the curtains/as the wind blew/
& the sun rays penetrated through your hidden walls/

it was early Saturday morning/when you reached out for me/
& I reached out for you/we were both holding on...holding on...holding on/
holding on with all of our might/as we drifted off.../
unto & away from unspoken passion/while/
sailing off to never...neverland...past the rising of the sun/
yet/feeling good all the way...down to the last drop/

it was early Saturday morning/& instead of coffee/instead of tea/
instead of me/you felt more alone...although your cup was already full!/
wondering/what it would be like to be on your own.../not/
because you held on, too!/but/because you let go.../but/

neither one of us really wanted too! hold on...that is!/even/
if it was good down to the very last drop.../then we soon woke up.../

it was early Saturday morning/& in a cold sweat/
realizing we both/
haven't even met.../   (Man wearing black exits and lights go dim)

(   )

                    (Enters men in red & beige along with the woman/Man wearing red starts to speaks)

I have a half a mind/to give U a piece of my mind.../

(he's talking crazy)/   (Man wearing beige)

"I would have married you/   (Woman starts to speaks)
but/baby...baby u don't have no degree..."/

(she's talking crazy)/   (Man wearing beige)

I don't know/   (Man wearing red)
maybe I love you.../
I don't know.../maybe I don't?/

(now maybe he's talking crazy)/   (Man wearing beige)

"If you were/   (Woman speaks)
a man...a real man/
you'll buy me this & you would want me to have that..."/
(she's still talking crazy)/   (Man wearing beige)

&/   (Man wearing red)
i'm mixed up/
mixed up cause' Sassy Sarah Vaughan.../
playing on the stereo in the other room/while/
my woman is in the bedroom/packing her things.../
to leave me one mo' time/

(& again he's talking crazy)/   (Man wearing beige)

yeah/   (Man wearing red)
Sarah's on my stereooooooooooo.../
& my woman is just standing there/this time looking crazy!/

&/   (Man wearing red moves towards the woman)
while/
I just sway my hips toward her way.../
& hum along with Sarah/putting a smile on her face.../
as we walk toward the bedroom/
& I start to help her unpack.../   (Man wearing red & the woman
                                                      run off stage laughing)

(   )

(Man wearing beige remains behind looking dumbfound/Enters man wearing orange, who starts to speak)

I ain't got no shame/no shame atoll!/
a broken heart maybe/but/
I/ain't got no shame/no shame atoll!/
cause/i'm just a po' ole black man/
down here on my bad luck/

'cause/   (Enters woman...she's pretending she' lookin' through a magazine)
u don't/
love me/love me no mo'/4 if u did/my heart wouldn't have been broken/
from no loving atol.../

i've done combed my nappy hair/
shined my dusty ole tennis shoes.../
twice, mind you girl!!!/   (Man wearing orange tries to get the woman total attention)
i even changed my funky/
funky/funky/
funky underwear...   (Woman giggles, yet she continues to read the magazine)
but/
'cause u don't love me/i'm now all dressed up/
without a got damn place to gooooooooo!/yeah!/
I/ain't got no shame/no shame atol!/
'cause u don't love me/
yet/i'ze keep'/comin' back 4 mo'/what/i'll tell u?/
no shame/
no shame atoll!/

          (Man wearing oranges walks over to the woman and they embraces & dashes off stage)

(   )

(Man wearing beige once again looks dumbfounded/as man wearing black enters & starts to speaks)

I/chipped my tooth/on a stale piece of peppermint candy cane/
candy cane, girl/from your candy jar.../

(Enters woman again, sexually playing with a candy cane hanging from her mouth)

I/said nothing/& kept right on chewing & sucking/sucking & chewing/
isn't love strange?/I/broke my favorite jazz recording/by the great ARCHIE SHEPP/
you/don't even like jazz/as a matter-of-fact...you can't stand J-A-Z-Z/
but/
you hummed it to me/   *(Woman walks over to him humming and they dance)*
& we slow dance/to "LUSH LIFE"/
& got drunk/& came down with an incredible high.../
isn't love strange?/

I/
kissed the cheek of an ole friend/   *(Man wearing black walks*
while we were out on the town last night/   *over to man wearing beige)*
you kissed the other cheek of my friend.../
saying:

"we shall all meet again...real soon."/   *(Women begins to speak)*

isn't love strange?/   *(Man wearing black continues speaking)*
I/needed peace & space/
space & peace.../& you sat across the room/& read a book/
softly humming, "LUSH LIFE"/while I fell off to sleep.../
isn't love strange?/
especially/
when it's all in a dream/   *(Woman slowly dances off stage humming...)*
'cause/
when I finally woke-up/girl...you were gone.../

(Man wearing black exits. Man wearing beige looks after him feeling sorry for him)

(   )

(Man wearing beige remains on stage once again; while man wearing brown enters speaking)

I/wanted an Essence Woman/instead/I got a Playgirl/
& my life has never been the same/   *(Woman enters)*
once/I granted u a peak at my Gentlemen Quarterly/

& u/told me it was quite charmin'/yet/we both knew/
we were Hustler's/through & through/out/2/get whatever we both could/
from whoever we could/whenever we could.../we/
only dreamt of Better Homes & Gardens/while/
remaining uncomfortable/within/these 4 walls of solitude/
u/I/we/us/called an apartment/as we continued to play house/

I wanted a Jet set centerfold or perhaps a Cosmopolitan girl/
an Ebony princess/instead/I had to settle for a bunny.../
who'd grown tired of her Playboy!/well/
girlfriend I've given up.../

u see/   (Man wearing beige)
now it's all about/
me & Blueboy/Black Inches & Machismo.../way Afterdark.../

       (Man wearing beige starts laughing as he blow kisses to man wearing brown,
        who starts to run from man wearing beige...who throws a magazine at him)

see that's life/when one lives/
their lives through pages of a few magazines.../   *(Man wearing brown*
                                            exits/lights dim)

(   )

       (Man wearing beige starts speaking as all the other men enters spot light is on man wearing beige)

in 1977 Alicia Bridges/sang about not catching a man/
by hanging out at a discotheque.../& loving the night life.../
child, I should have listen/as I left the dance floor of the Buttermilk Bottom/
a club in the Tribeca area of NYC/

       (Man wearing blue, while the lights fade in on two men groping one another in the semi-dark)

in 1979 his first love held him in the corner of Peter Rabbits,/
a bar/club in NYC/& played with his innocent emotions/

in 1981/   (Man wearing beige)
while Grace Jones sang, "*I Need A Man*"/
I was trying to get one...which is the story of my life.../
while dancin' at Le Circus/the New Horizon and/or Catch One Disco'/
in Los Angeles.../only to end back up in NYC with the Nasty Girls/
ridin' around in long white limo's/from uptown at Studio 54/

to the downtown Paradise Garage on Kings Street in Greenwich Village/

(Man wearing orange & another man walks towards man wearing beige as they...
continue to walk off together...while man wearing beige places on wig & high heels)

in 1983 my lover at that time left me for another/
while I became a *"Private Dancer"* at Better Days/
a club on 49th & 8th Avenue in NYC.../
replacing my innocence with high heels & wigs/

in 1984/   *(Man wearing purple)*
a lover at the time/
met death at the door of the Nickel Bar/
a club on 72nd Street & Columbus Avenue.../
& never came home/instead.../
he/i/we/started looking at
the *"Man in the mirror"*/   *(All the men hold up mirrors checking themselves out...)*

in 1986/   *(Man wearing blue)*
a new love & he exchanged/
body fluid in the bathroom stall of Lorretta's, in Atlanta, GA/
not one condom/
was used among them!/

in 1987/   *(Man wearing beige returns alone...)*
at a bar called Pegasus/
in Macon, Georgia.../
Whitney Houston & I both sang *"I get so emotional"*/
which showed me/that love & being in love/could never be for keeps/
when found in a bar or discotheque/no matter what State.../
you were currently living in/

in 1989/   *(Man wearing brown)*
Keller's Bar/
on NYC Westside hwy/
had don on new faces/faces that dominated the bar scene.../
while some *"children"*/of the/
70s, 80s were at home hooked up to IV's & wearing diapers/

in 1990/   *(Man wearing blue)*
the funky grove of/
club/house/techno music.../music/that throughout the clubs.../

at a bar called Heaven in England.../& in Braxton, England/
is where he met Bono from U-2/& Frankie Crooker from NYC Radio Station WBLS/
while dancin' on the discotheque floor of the Frigid.../
& Big Jim's in Adana, Turkey/or/at Ankar's Aeroport nightclub.../
which opted for rap music.../& the english chaps/
& Turkish boys continue to dance with death.../
while "*blaming it on the rain, rain, rain,*"/see not only was Manilla/Vanilla/
in denial/but so was Uncle Sam/with his slogan of "*Don't Ask, Don't Tell*"/
something universal among/men/I guess...men in or out of uniforms.../

in 1992/   (Man wearing orange)
the term fag hag/
became a thing of the pass/as the boys started hanging uptown/
at places like Doll's/on B'way & 141st Street/
& or Joe L's/on B'way 192nd Street/
with out their cover fish...cover fisheeeees is...or are/
for those who don't know/what cover fish...is.../
cover fish-are girls/women used for dating purposes only.../
or at the Delta or Tracks'/in Washington, DC/
where/
he still couldn't get no man   (Looks over at the man wearing beige...)

in 1996/   (Man wearing black)
& back on/American soil the "children"/
were having sex/some protected/some unprotected/
on the third floor of King's in Chelsea/
& behind curtains in the boxing ring at Champs/both/
while stuffing $1.00 bills/in the cheeks of muscle boys dancer/
who use to be a male hustlers for .50.../in the Time Sq. peep shows/
way before "*Giuliani Times rolled on in...*"/
which/i guess one can call, that progress.../
which takes us back/20 years ago to the year 1977/
when Alicia Bridges sang about her not being able to catch no man by hanging/
out at no discotheque/
"*...well I believe in the boggie/
but loving is really my game/*   (Man wearing beige starts
                                                        singin' to everyone' dismay...)

(At this time all the men are running from him thinking the he has gone
crazy or something about themselves will be revealed...?)

Alicia, girl.../
I/ should have listen!/

Alicia, girl.../
I/should have listen!/

Alicia, girl.../
I/should have listen!/

Lord, knows...child/
Alicia girl.../
I should have listen!/

but did I? No!/
yet/in 1997 I had found myself/
now/
hangin' out uptown/
at the Lenox Lounge on 125th Str./
& even in the Bronx/at the new funky Warehouse/
right off of the Grand Concourse/
dancing for my life.../
dancing because/
of /my love one' death/dancing in order to find peace/
dancing between these internal wars/
dancing & fighting with my very own demons/
dancing with men/men in which/I still adore/
yet/
not/one of those men/will I ever love.../
like my first love/
a man who had played with/
my innocent emotions.../
as I continue to dance/
to/Ms. Chaka Khan's latest hit "Never missed your water..."

          (Man wearing beige starts singing a new song...
            has he walks off stage. Lights fade to a soft dimmer...)

(   )

woke up this mornin'/   *(Man wearing green enters and steps into the spot light)*
(tick, tock, tick, tock)

(All the tick, tock, tick, tock are heard from backstage by the other cast members...)

stirred from the right/
then/I/stirred to the left
(tick, tock, tick, tock)

there/I/
was with so much confusion laying beside me/
from the night before/
(tick, tock, tick, tock)

was it the stranger lying next to me.../
next to me/
in my bed/
(tick, tock, tick, tock)

(Lights come up featuring a semi-nude man laying on the floor wrapped up in sheets
...lights go back down...)

oh! my, my, my.../
(tick, tock, tick, tock)

woke up this mornin'/
(tick, tock, tick, tock)

with a complete stranger in my bed.../
(tick, tock, tick, tock)

guest i'll had better lay back down.../
(tick, tock, tick, tock)

in order/to get reacquainted/with this stranger in my bed.../

(Man wearing green steps into the spot light, semi-nude...
They both rises and embraces each other, lights out...they exit)

(   )

we awoke/   *(Man wearing beige speaks while another*
afraid to say good morning/   *man appears to be getting dressed)*
was it/because of the odor & taste of each other sex in our mouths?/
but/hey/we loved each other/last night/
what's a little tasteful odor/of morning breathe uhm!/

we rose/this morning/
touching each other/
rather/
I touched & you just laid there/but/hey/we like one another/
don't we?/
we'll work something out.../
see life had/took upon a new meaning/
for the both of us this morning/

a meaning of.../
cleaning out house/& setting down/some basic rules/
for each other/but/only in/each other's minds/
but hey again what remains/
unsaid/will come to light...surely one day/
hey/let's pull back the curtain/& drawback the sheets/
& with the help of God's sunlight/
perhaps/we can both re-examine each other genitals/
by counting the spilled semen between the both of us.../
I estimate/2 million!/
what/
a waste you say?/
I/agree, now i'm sorry but you must leave.../

(Man exits, while man wearing beige is laying among the sheets & pillows on the floor...lights go down)

(   )

                    (Man wearing beige raises as man wearing white enters & starts to speaks)

numbers jotted down/
from whores met on Saturday night at some nearby bar/
empty doublement foil wrappers/
with the whores gum, still in tact.../
that I've kept for safe keeping/
while I gave her a load of my very own/   (Man wearing beige exits in disgusted)

a few pennies/nickel & dimes/for she was only a $2.00 whore.../
fake i.d.,/fake eyelashes,/one rubberband...
for what.../who the hell knows?
one loose joint/yep/that about covers it/
& you thought the hugh bulge/
in the front of my jeans.../

was cause I was happy to see you again tonight?/
don't kid yourself.../
whore/
my love for your love tonight/fell out through a hole in my back pocket.../

(Man wearing white exits...stage right, while showing a hole in his back pocket)

(   )

I should have seen it a mile way/   *(Man wearing red enters...)*
for/it was as clear/
as having no tree on Christmas day/
your love wasn't here to stay!/
I should have known/
from past experience & common sense/
that your pockets were so heavy laden/
from/having been filled with so many lies, on top of mo' lies.../
I should have known/
I should have known/
Lord, knows/
I should have known.../
for you see/
there were signs all over town/that/
you were heading for a great fall/while/
using me as your soft cushion.../   *(Man wearing red exits stage right...)*

(   )

besides/   *(Man wearing yellow enters stage left)*
a paper cup/
there's/a tiny/sharp piece of glass/
besides/
a tiny/
sharp piece of glass/there's a plastic paper cup/
we've drank from the paper cup/
& we've spit up bits & pieces/
of what's left of yesterday' romance/
now/
that our time is up.../
U must see/that today my love has gone astray/
causin' pieces of glass/

to fill each of our tiny/plastic paper cups/
with memories of a simple love/
that has gone astray.../   (Man wearing yellow exits...stage right)

(   )

i'm sorry/   (Man wearing green from stage right
you're sorry/   almost bumping into man wearing yellow)
sorry seems to be the sorriest words/
for both you & I/
we're so sorry/
that/being happy/being thankful/had just up & walked away/
leaving/
two sorry souls/crying a river full of sorries/
& watching their tears roll into a endless pit/
that/never seems to fill up/
yet somehow/
it doesn't matter/these bunch of sorries
that have been withdrawn/
from everyone/of our unsecured riverbanks/
teachin' us the true/
meaning/
of the phrase: no deposit, no returns.../   (Man wearing green exits stage right)

(   )

I/   (Man wearing beige enters stage left)
wanted a black & white/
sweet romance/
the kind of romance/
that/
allows 1/2 dance...
I/
wanted to love a colour/
just/as long/as that colour does not leave me/
feeling/
so black & blue.../   (Lights go out as man wearing beige exits...stage right)

(   )

        (Enters woman who walks towards center of the stage as she starts to speak)

like a cat in the heat of the night/
I can find my very own way/
only/
if/u just stay away!/

it' the act/   (Man wearing white enters...very cautiously)
of u coming around here/
wearing/
that/silly ole smile/
flicking on & turning off my got damn lights/
your timin'.../
your timin' just ain't right/
do u/
really think/
i'd want to see u/   (Man wearing black enters...very slowly, too!)
fake those crocodile tears.../
tears glisting in the moonlight/
soaking up my newly designer fresh clean sheets/
& steaming up my squeaky clean Windex shine/
only makes me think/
u/my brother, my lover, my man...can't be genuine/
yeah/
your crooked smiles/your backstabbing lies.../
my/what hard rain falls against my window pane/

(Enters man wearing blue carryin' an umbrella and starts to open it
but the woman stops him...)

damn it.../God only knows/how much/I can't stand the rain/
my pain instills such a flashing delight/
as u watched me drown in your make believe crocodile tears/
the day light blinds me/into seeing to much at night/
could it be the wild bunch/
you started hanging out with/just to get away
from me...?/   (Enters man wearing purple)
my entire life is hung up for your hang ups/
& like a jigsaw puzzle picture frame/
& the daily dust rags/
that I used to rid myself of you.../
the green glad bags/   (Woman starts handin' out large green Glad trash bags)
that i'll like to tie/

you up in.../& when I'm through with the painful thought of all of this/
it tend' to make me mad/as I just keep/
it to myself/
& just continued/   (Man wearing brown looks sort of surprised)
to take out/
the morning trash'/
along with your mess...you cheatin'...low down trifling fool/

        (Woman starts throwing their personal things at them, and the
              men start placing their items into the green bags...)

now that the entire house is cleared/
would you like to wait to fill my broken cup of heart breaks?/
yes/my vision isn't so clear these days/
perhaps a 45, 60 maybe 100 watts should hit the spot!/
as I drawback the iron curtain of my broken heart/
only to make sure it's no holiday dressed up turkey/
i'm serving to this po' fool/who's been flirting.../

you/   (Man wearing orange enters and helps the others collects their belongings)
see/
someone else'/name was mentioned last night/
while in a heat of passion.../
yeah,/just forget to pay ConEd & you too/my dear/
then/will see the light...while alone & sittin' in the dark.../

        (Woman exits, leaving all the men standing there clueless...while the lights go out)

(   )

you/   (Man wearing green enters)
thought I knew/
I thought you knew come to find out we both ended-up/
singing the fuckin' blues.../
life's strange.../
so got damn/strange.../
it's a wonder that the phoenix could have risen so high above dry ashes/
& you can only find interest in bringing me down/

woman/   (Enters woman)
all I ask of u...is why? why? why?/
why must you insist on telling me lies/

you thought I knew/
I thought you knew/come to find out/we both ended-up/
singin' the fuckin' blues.../
it's been said many times before/
that foxes are very sly/that God may shed his grace upon thee/
that/money is the root of all evil/
& we must all par-take of it's fruit, bitter as it maybe/
& that blood is thicker than water/
yet/
your cup of my blood/has runneth/over & over & over again, again/
yeah/
all God's chillus got soul/
then/
why in the hell/come Sunday mornin'/
you/
lose yours?/   *(Woman and man wearing green exits together,*
                                              while he starts shaking his head...)

(   )

you/   *(Man wearing orange enters)*
worked/
your voodoo magic/
now I am your voodoo slave/
you're my hunter/
& I am/your prey/& I shall love you to my grave/
'cause girl your/
love is killing me.../   *(Man wearing orange exits)*

(This poem can be omitted for brevity...)

I   *(Man wearing yellow enters)*

lying my warm hands against the nape of your neck/
your fingers gently caresses the tip of my moist & eager tongue/

as/   *(Man wearing blue enters)*
time passed/
the moisture from sweet dew drops/
fell upon our embracing bodies/
creating a heat of passion/

as each hairs.../   (Man wearing white enters)
hairs on each of our bodies parts/
stands on its edges/
I/wonder does it have anything to do with the current of our passion?/

the motions/   (Man wearing blue enters)
of dark shadows dancin'/
in the flickering candlelight/

as/   (Man wearing yellow enters)
I explore the walls/
of your lustrous beehive/

& as/   (Man wearing white)
if in a dream/
we/
both fell/off to sleep.../

yet/   (Man wearing blue)
we will/meet again/
perhaps/while encased.../
captured in a ole lover' time warp!/
or/madly & presently in love with each other/

in/   (Man wearing yellow)
a bell jar/
tossed & looking out.../
out into/
a bottomless pit/

yet/   (Man wearing white)
we continue to dream/of our needin' to love & beloved/

as/   (Man wearing yellow)
we floated/
floated on a bed of entangled limbs/

limbs/   (Man wearing blue)
that had fallen/
from life's cut down branches/

then/   (Man wearing white)

dreaming/
of climbing to the climax.../
a climax of all climax'/while pretending to be happy.../
some of the time.../most of the time.../yet, not all the time.../

as/   (Man wearing yellow)
we both straighten out our unhappy smiles/

at/   (Man wearing blue)
one time/
they/were such pretty smiles/

yet with a monkey/   (Man wearing white)
on each of our backs/
we both/dared to jump/
jump into the sack/

the sunshine/   (Man wearing yellow)
has been locked.../
locked out/from the both of us.../
for so long/with no key to be found/

leaving you & me/   (Man wearing blue)
hanging/from unfulfilled/
dream/
unmatched passion/

as/   (Man wearing white)
we continue/
to fumble in the dark/

   All the man speak in unison while actin' a sexual act/which leads to a climax & then they exits)

come & hold/
hold on/hold on/hold on to.../hold on to my arched back.../

II

...bite/   (Man wearing black enters)
into my neck/
& allow me to french curl your natural state of mind/

help me/help me to change prime time/
into our midnight hour rendezvous/love making/takes time/
hey don't stop!
hey why did you stop?/
oh, I see.../now/it' your hair that' standin' on its ends/
could it be/could/it be...the current?/could it be/could/
it be...the current?/or is it the word love?/
yeah the word love that' it.../
the word love/
that/
draws you so far away.../   (Man wearing black exit)

(   )

all wrapped up/   (Man wearing brown enters)
from/
head to toe/
yet/with no one to be given too!/

all wrapped up/
with/my share of both love & hate.../
wonderin' why/
I am always in such a fixed state?/

all wrapped up/
always/wanting mo'/
yet having to make much ado/
with/muchless/than/I have bargain for/

all wrapped up/
hey/what about u...?/

(Man wearing brown looks out into the audience/then exits stage right)

(This poem can be omitted for brevity...)

&/   (Man wearing red enters stage left)
how was your day?/
did you wake up singin'/did you wake up dancin'/
dancin' to that same ole familiar tune?/
did you sip coffee from a lover' cup?/
did you take a nibble from their burnt toast?/

or did you just smiled/
& say: "it' goin' to be a great day..."/
well/if you did/
my dear/perhaps we should have a serious talk/
once/you finally wake the fuck up!/
now/
I'll repeat/
how was your day?/   (Man wearing red runs off stage left)

(This poem can be omitted for brevity...)

like spilled milk/   (Man wearing beige enters)
that/
leaves stains upon one' coffee table/
I found markin' of someone else' body...imprinted on my soil sheets/
like a reader seeks a good book/
we read each other from cover to cover/
yet/
wandering if we really knew one another!/
like a chef seeks a well equipped kitchen/a kitchen filled/w/ pots & pans/
& racks of day ole spices/
I'd cooked up an image of you/
& then sat down/& ate it alone.../never satisfied & hungry still/
like a singer seeks a good note/
I wanted to transform ourselves into a beautiful symphony/
yet/you opted for a solo.../
like a musician seeks his rum & coke/
I found my tongue flickering, darting in & out of your thighs/
working it' way up your shaft,/
only to stop at the suckin' sounds,/
as I sip moisture from your navel,/all the time,/i'm a thinkin'.../
have I found the right key?/once again/asking myself the question of.../
that/if this is the likeness of being in love/
then I/
must ask you to leave & find me a new love.../   (Man wearing beige exits)

(This poem can be omitted for brevity...)

I

(Enters men wearing black, red, blue & brown...man wearing black starts to speak)

Isaac Hayes sang:
"...a man must be a man..." & "it's a man's world..."/
came from the Godfather of Soul James Brown/
with a big payback/

I/   (Man wearing blue)
am told/
that/
brother Donny Hathaway stated:
"...if I ever hurt you...you know I hurt myself as well"/

Yeah/   (Man wearing brown)
I've been there, done that/
& I even brought the got damn t-shirt!/

I've listened/   (Man wearing red)
to other black men.../
black men telling me what's it all about.../
all about/when it comes to being a man & black, too!/

but/   (Man wearing black)
some men/
cover up their problems, hurts & their anger/
just by claimin'not to have any problems/atol/or even perhaps/
not being part of the whole problem themselves.../
as brother Thomas A. Parham has.../
stated: "...as black males, we have become partners in our demise."

it's/   (Man wearing blue)
everyone else fault:racism/sexism/finance.../

& yet/   (Man wearing red)
no women has the right to put in her say so/
unless/it's with a warm smile & lovin' arms/
lovin' arms to protect her man from hurtin'/
from hurtin' himself/from hurtin' her/from hurtin' the entire world...

sister/ (Man wearing black)
Nikki Giovanni said:
"...if a man refuses to be a man...
it's alright, i'll love him any way." (Woman speaks)

sister Nikki.../ (Man wearing brown)
where/were you/
when I needed you the most?/

a man is a man/ (Man wearing black)
when his worldly/
problems & life/numerous pitfalls, stormy as they maybe.../
engulfs him & he doesn't allow it to eat at his:
personhood/nor challenge/nor destroy his manhood/

but/ (Man wearing blue)
stands rooted/
& ready to press on/& if his woman/
doesn't offer the silent warm smiles/& loving arms/
& just ups & walks away/

then/ (Man wearing red)
he'll just have to stand on his own/

yeah/ (Man wearing black)
a man's problem/
must be dealt with in a manly sort of way/
that/only a man (white or black) can look back/
&/say like ole Blu' Eyes/& say: "I did it my way."

II

a man is only human/ (Man wearing brown)
& he/has & will continue to have his fair share of give & take/
& if he lives/to become ole & grey/

he'll have many mo'/ (Man wearing red)
to his very dying day/

from (Man wearing blue)
eating puntang/to frying catfish/both he caught from hangin'/
out with/the boys/on Saturday night/

or/   (Man wearing red as he looks around for the man wearing beige...)
having/
to lately don on a tight pair of Calvin Klein' jeans/

then/   (Man wearing beige enters)
leaving/the lil woman home/
while/her man/cruised the city streets/
way pass midnight/
he say: "...just to clear his head."/
while/
catching some handsome fairy...cruising his trade/
as night/becomes day/& lately wondering/
why/the hell not?/
could the media have taken the AIDS crisis/
way/
out of contexts?   (Man wearing beige looks over at the man wearing red)

III

see now/   (Man wearing black)
that the IRS has a $86,000,000.00 tax debt/
here I am a black man on this Christmas Eve/
with only a dime to my name/& no love one to share a red cents of it with/

since/   (Man wearing brown)
my woman done walked off/
leaving me so Black & Blu'/

yes/   (Man wearing black)
not only does/
colored girls, consider suicide.../
when their rainbow' just ain't' all what it's expected to be/

yeah/   (All the men in unison as they dash off stage in various directions...)
some of us fellas bleed, too...

(This poem can be omitted for brevity...)

if/   (Enters men wearing yellow and purple...man wearing purple starts to speak)
I can only/
roll it/roll it/between my fingertips

if/   (Man wearing yellow)
it can only be held/in the palm of my hands/
my/what a lovely thing it would be/

if/   (Man wearing purple)
I can touch it/
yet not have it crumble in the palm of my hand/
for it's as old as father time/

if/   (Man wearing yellow)
it had only a pleasant scent/
like a rainy afternoon/in the springtime/

my/   (Man wearing purple)
what a lovely/thing it would be/

if/   (Man wearing yellow)
black/the color of my skin/
could only be looked upon as a blessing/
rather/
then the burden it has become/

if/   (Man wearing purple)
man/woman/woman/man/man/man & woman/woman/
could only embrace one another/in these here tryin' times/

my/   (Man wearing yellow)
what a lovely thing it would be/

if/   (Both men say this in unison)
I could/
only shape all these things between my ten little fingers/
my, my, my/what a lovely thing this colorful world/
would be.../

        (Man wearing purple exit stage right & man wearing yellow exit left)

(This poem can be omitted for brevity...)

we built sandcastles/   (Man wearing white enter)
along the seashores/
you took the east wing/& I silently accepted your decision/
(while feeling defeated), to hang out in the west wing/

nevertheless I settled for the west wing/
the north,/the south, was left up to both our distant/
& long forgotten/hopes & dreams.../

(Man wearing white freezes in his place...Until the lights dim down)

(This poem can be omitted for brevity...)

I

(Enter men wearing beige, purple, orange & black, red...man wearing beige speaks)

now that Donna Summer has made her come back/
with "Dinner with Gershwin"/   (Man wearing beige starts to sing the song)

& Madonna has taught me about capitalism/
by stealing the creativity energy of a dying population/
& movements of both black & latino gay men, with her rendition of voguin'/
hollywood had forgotten/
that/the dance craze stemmed from rival dance competition/
between openly gay men/
in the late 70s & early 80s/gay men/who didn't wish to mess/
up their jerri curl's & high top fade/
against the boys/who were/
on the (down low) or not totally out of the closet.../
(there use to be an ole sayin'...today's trade...is tomorrow' competition)/
boys on the D.L. (a 90s expression)/
who dance at gay clubs in NYC.../& breakdancin' one moment/
& the next moment was beatin' up gay men in dark alley'...after reachin' a climax.../
boys who/danced at clubs,/like Better Days/
or/Peter Rabbits on the West End Hwy./
Tracks & the Paradise Garage/& the Ice Palace on 57th Str./
which later became the Silver Shadow/
for the straight kids.../

see both/   (Man wearing red)
Donna & Madonna/
listed a host of names in their recording/
in/which/one has a line that does: "ladies with an attitude..."/

well/   (Man wearing beige)
yes/

I have just/that/an attitude!/
an/attitude/because/few/if any person of color/was/mentioned in either recording'/
if I'm wrong/then/pig could most certainly do fly/

yet/   *(Man wearing orange)*
I/can remember back in the day'/

when I'd/   *(Man wearing purple)*
pitched a number of pennies/
with/the best of the crowd/
Carmichael/Evers & even Bro. Miles/just to name a few/

I/   *(Man wearing red)*
drank/
bootleg whiskey & watched other black po' folks/walk the talk & danced/the Haarlem shuffle/

in/   *(Man wearing black)*
some hole-in-the-wall/
10cent bar on what is now/called Malcolm X Blvd./

I've looked/   *(Man wearing red)*
for cheap enthrallments/
just to pass another/Saturday night up in Haarlem/

I/   *(Man wearing black)*
ate ole jim crow/for Sunday's brunch/

I/   *(Man wearing red...music "Roots" by Odyssey, again.)*
ate Mr. & Mrs. Segregation/
& threw-up their children's children/
& called them integration by Monday morning for lunch/

I then set myself/   *(Man wearing beige)*
right on down & had tea/with some British Queen/
it could have been one of hollywood's tv's/
from the drag strip ball/
who/knows, you've seen one Queen's ball/
you've seen them all/
now that "*Paris has burned*"/
for/Ms. Livingston, is another one/
who capitalize off of dying young gay men.../

then/   (Man wearing orange)
when the party/
ended at the Savoy/
I/
ended-up without my morning cup of coffee/

see/   (Man wearing black)
the coffee shop was bombed/
the day before.../

&/   (Man wearing red)
I only had one nickel/
to my got damn name/

maybe/   (Man wearing purple)
a dime/
thinking/perhaps a TV dinner will suit me just the same

I/   (Man wearing black)
then/
ended-up/with nothing to show for my people'/

my/   (Man wearing red)
people/
who were out there fighting for the cause/

but/   (Man wearing orange)
instead/I/sat myself.../
down to watch some news

news/   (Man wearing beige)
about my brothers & sisters with empty pockets/
empty pockets that once was filled with dreams/
watching/their broken spirits/dark bruises & cuts & bumps/

bumps/   (Man wearing red)
from white officers billy clubs/

noting/   (Man wearing black)
that/some of the black ones weren't any better/
in up holding the laws/

seen/   (Man wearing orange)
a sister chased down/chased down like a dog/

while/   (Man wearing purple)
holding on/
to what was once a poster board/which read: "civil rights for everyone..."
another/   (Man wearing black)
brother was talking about cold cell blocks/
with paper thin beds & being held over/
from yesterday's afternoon cities riots/

while/   (Man wearing red)
riotin'/
in the city jails/
that/held a crowd of my people/
once again in bondage.../

II

but/   (All the men say in unison)
I/
remember:

when/   (Man wearing beige)
I sat in on peace talks along/
with Frederick Douglass,/Wm. DuBois,/Gandhi/
& a man named Dr. King/

I/   (All the men say in unison)
remember:

reading the thought'/   (Man wearing black)
of James "Jimmy" Arthur Baldwin,/
Marcus Garvey/& a woman named Barbara Jordan/

I/   (All the men say in unison...)
remember:

having heated discussion/   (Man wearing purple)
with women about women/
& their equal rights/
women like: Nikki Giovanni/Angela Y. Davis & sister Maya Angelou, too!/

three women/   (Man wearing orange)
who'd dared to tell both black & white men/
what they could & can not do for them & to them.../

telling/   (Man wearing beige)
it to their faces/
yet/
lovin' them all the same/when those same men turned their backs on them.../

women/   (Man wearing purple)
who called them lil boys with toys guns/
& lil boys with a brains for a third leg...ruinin' many a male egooooooos!!!/

I/   (All the man say in unison)
remember:

singin'   (Man wearing black)
protest songs/
with the touch of the blue'/while marchin' right along side/
the spirit of Lady Day & Bessie Smith/
& Madam Nina Simone, singin' "to be young, gifted & black..."

three/   (Man wearing beige)
women/
with a gentle but soulful & powerful & stroking voices/
Madam Simone/please/come on home/the city of Baltimore misses you/

I/   (All the men say in unison)
remember:

struttin' my stuff/   (Man wearing red)
from the cut rug tunes of The Duke/
The Count/& yes/oh, yes/The Godfather/& the Queen of Soul/

Aretha!/   (Man wearing beige)
Aretha!/
Aretha! "yes...don't play that song for me..."
unless you're able to keep it real...
dinner with Gershwin, sister Donna what in the hell/
were you & Sister Brenda Russell thinking of...?/

not/   (Man wearing red)
only have the two of you done lost your got damn minds?/

but/   (Man wearing black)
you two/have/lost your/roots.../

dinner/   (Man wearing red)
with Gershwin my ass!/

as/   (Man wearing beige)
I was saying.../

I/   (All the men say in unison)
remember:

studying/   (Man wearing orange)
the four R's/

reading/   (Man wearing purple)

'riting/   (Man wearing black)

'rithmetic/   (Man wearing red)

& religion/   (Man wearing beige, all the other man look at them)

along with the best of them.../   (Man wearing orange)
DuBois,/Carver,/even Einstein & ole Father Divine/
with fingernails & all/

I/   (All the men say in unison)
remember:

learning to dance/   (Man wearing beige)
a step or two by sweepin up Ms. Jamierson/
Mr. Miller & graceful brother Alvin Ailey/off their feet/
while all of us stomped & liddy-hop at the Cotton Club/

I/   (All the men say in unison)
remember:

kissing the hollywood/   (Man wearing black)
silver screens whenever/
divas: like Dorothy Dandrige, Lena Horne/
or sister Diahann Carroll would ever appear/

I/   *(All the men say in unison)*
remember:

playing/   *(Man wearing orange)*
many roles on stages of the world/
in productions written
by Ossie Davis, Lorraine Hansberry & even a white dude
by the name of Wm. Shakespeare

just/   *(Man wearing black)*
to prove Othello needed no dark Egyptian make-up/
to get over or to pass through/

pass/   *(Man wearing red)*
through/
the/
for colored signs/
left over from yesterday's riots/

riots/   *(Man wearing black)*
that/held my people wrapped up in bondage.../

III

then/   *(Man wearing beige)*
after all of this/I/attended Sunday services/
only to thank God/for getting us through it all/

& how about you?/   *(In unison...addressin' the audience...)*

now/   *(Man wearing purple)*
that/Donna Summer's made a comeback/
& is now having dinner with Gershwin

perhaps/   *(Man wearing black)*
having left over from yesterday's bondage that held.../

that held.../   *(All the men are chanting)*
that held.../
that held.../

my people/   (Man wearing black)
together for all of these years.../
In/   (Man wearing beige, who starts to vogue)
spite/
of Madonna & Ms. Livingston' capitalist, money making scheme'/

do I sound bitter?/   (Man wearing red)

uhm,/   (Man wearing beige)
just ask Lil Richard.../

then/
you tell me...?/

(In unison...then they all freeze...& the lights softens...)

15 INTERMISSION...

ACT III...

Movements in time...Man-to-Man Relationships

NOW...(90s moving toward the new millennium)

> "*When the book comes out it may hurt you-but in order for me to do it, it had to hurt me first. I can only tell you about yourself as much as I can face about myself.*"-**James BROTHA 2 BROTHA**
>
> *-A1-Black Elite Chat Line, Internet Source Unknown*

(   )

NOW...

(Enters men wearing white, yellow, brown, green & blue & they all freeze until it's their turn to speak)

I

(Woman speaks with a English accent through out this monologue...she now
the homeless woman, who rides NYC subway askin' for change)

"...can you spare some change, please!"

Uptown: Gunhill Road/   (Man wearing black)
Haarlem U.S.A., 42nd Street/Time Square/
perhaps even the Greenwich Village piers/

Downtown: Bay Ridge/   (Man wearing red)
Bed-Stuy, Howard Beach.../
maybe one can take a far-out-ride on the round-robin "CC" train/
& back to nowhere on the "A" train/

yes with a token in one hand/   (Man wearing blue)
& in the other hand.../no place to go/
so you just ride from one end of Mott Avenue/out-in-Far Rockaway/
to/207th Street in Manhattan/just a po' lost soul/looking for space.../

oh/   (Man wearing green)
yes there's always choices.../
there' a choice to go to school/a choice to go to work/
or just go back home.../

yet our choice/   (Man wearing yellow)
was to go up to the candy man.../yeah, the candy man/
up on 123rd Street/to cop some smoke & a lil coke/
you know Haarlem wouldn't mind/
you see the Senator's lil boy made it way up here/only to go back higher/
then his father' little white lies/lies of not being down by a creek/
& with a dead white lady, too?/

but/   (Man wearing brown)
maybe i'm sayin' just a lil bit to much/

when/I start to challenge a public figure.../a public figure w/no right balls/
& his mama has only one left tit/

II

or better yet/ (Man wearing purple)
crack lines can lead one to Lenox Avenue/
(now called Malcolm X Blvd.)/Brother Malik Haik Shabazz/
must be rolling over in his grave/right beside/
Adam Clayton Powell Jr. & Frederick Douglass/2 men.../
who have both been reduced 2 just numbers.../
numbers called 7th Avenue & 8th Avenues.../

Uptown/ (Man wearing orange)
at the Apollo/there's a crowd there every Wednesday night.../
the night they call amateur night (*sort of deja vu of the Roman Empire arena*)/
in which/their boos & laughter can cut/can cut just as deep as a gladiators sword/

all of this/ (Man wearing beige)
I/envision while riding *Ms. "A" Train & bad-ass Mr. "D" train*/
which by the way.../can lead 1/2/the point of:

(*Man wearing white, as the woman enters...& acts out drama with the men*)

"*Boom, boom, boom...give me your money you old bitch/or/
i'll blow your motherfuckin' brains out*"/

4 the 10 year old/ (Man wearing black)
didn't know/
that the 86 year old great-great grandmother/who/was/
now being called a bitch/paved the way/
for him to go to McDonald's & ride the front of a city bus/

that 10 yr old.../ (Man wearing red)
he shot her/shot her in cold blood/
just because she was moving to slow for his fast ass.../

III

while on the No. 1 Train the other day/ (Man wearing blue)
no one saw a thang/nor said a thang/

nor heard the mother of 6/being called a bitch.../
by a 32 year old grand mother/with her 14 year child/
& 9 month old grand-child/all because/the mother of 6/
sat on the 32 year old grand mother's Macy's bag.../a Macy's bag of stolen goods.../

at 7:30 p.m./   (Man wearing green)
during rush hour/no-less/no one had better dare to look up.../
look up.../from their "Color Purple," "Waiting to Exhale" or
"Invisible Life" novels/NY Times/Essence/
or Rolling Stones/ViBe/Source magazines/
as the 12 year old gangster bitch/
lit' up a joint.../lit' up a joint on the "F" Train/I kid you not...

no one paid much attention/   (Man wearing yellow)
when the 10 year old'/
loaded pistol went off & shot the young woman w/child in her womb.../

no one said a word/   (Man wearing brown)
because she was holding/another child's hand.../
a child who had nappy edges/& the dying woman/
who was with the child & holding that child' hand/was a dirty bleach blond/

all they saw/   (Man wearing purple)
while riding out to Bensonhurst, B'klyn/
was another nigger lover/

yeah/   (Man wearing orange)
this is NYC in transit/watch/watch/
watch the closing dooooooooooors/

no one reached out/   (Man wearing beige)
to the young Puerto Rican girl/
who was pushed to her death/
by a deranged homeless person/late at night/
while ridin' on the "B" Train/heading into Dekalb Avenue/

or the old Irish woman/   (Man wearing white)
who was stabbed to her death/
as she made her why to payin' her senior citizen discount/
towards those heavenly pearly gates/up in heb-ben.../

IV

i can remember when the fair was .75/   (Man wearing black)
now it's a $1.50/yeah, man/the tunnel of hell/
may cost mo'/but/it's still the same/nothing' changed/
but our wardrobes & bad hairdos & fucked up attitudes/
$1.50 doesn't pay/   (Man wearing red)
4 our 9-2-5/when/we are all doing 9-2-life/
or better/yet/becoming a prisoner within our very own homes/
or on cell block 4/deja vu of times spent at Riker's Island/

but/   (Man wearing blue)
hey/you think you're soooooo...cooooool/
walking around with your G.E.D./
which truly means: great errancies dummy/

& the minimum wage/   (Man wearing green)
isn't enuf/
for your daily high/& going home is a journey of 500 years ago!

hey/   (Man wearing yellow)
mutherfucker.../
instead of drinking that fucken' Ole English/
or St. Isles' & smoking those got damn Newports...& rolled up trees/
shit/always buyin' or bumming a got damn loosely from me.../

i told you to leave/   (Man wearing brown)
that damn basketball court alone/
& learn how to swim/right along with those white boys/
from Bensonhurst, B'klyn/

4...1...day/   (Man wearing purple)
you my brother/just might have to swim across the ocean/
beggin' to be let back into the Congo/
that's/
if the real Africans would let you?/

hey, look over yonder.../   (Man wearing beige)

if you can see pass/   (Man wearing orange)
the crowded train/there' a man in his mid-40s/
& God only knows he should know better/

but/ (Man wearing beige)
he's bustin' a nut against a 13 year old/
school girl's rear end/or/is that a grown woman/
or perhaps it's a lil boy/hell these days/
one could never tell for sure…just ask Father Flangan?/

yeah!/ (Man wearing orange)
this is NYC in transit/watch/watch/
watch the closing dooooooooors…/
this is NYC in transit/watch the closing dooooooooors…/this is…this is…this is…/

your family & friends/ (Man wearing black)
when you're able to find them between court appearances…/
they all have taken a ride on the Reading/
but did not pass go/& did not collected their $200/instead/
they/went straight to jail/& so now you are ridin' & trickin' or treatin'/
for this is the era of the give me generation…twice removed…/

a generation/ (Man wearing red)
that/kills whenever the mood strikes them/
a generation/
that replaced their hoola hoops skirts & Barbie dolls…/
for now they have become real life G.I. Joes & Mary Janes/
killin' whenever…killin' whenever…killin' whenever…/
the mood/strikes them…/

V

I once was young/ (Man wearing black)
thank God not that foolish…/my brothers & sisters/
we need everyone of you to become: excellent students/nurturing mothers/
present & responsible fathers/supporting sisters/& willing & able brothers/
caring uncles/loving aunts/& watchful & givin' grandparents…/

for this/ (Man wearing blue)
we must instill in all of our youth' today/
to become: lawyers instead of prisoners/
doctors instead of Friday night/
& Saturday morning patients/
directors/producers & writers/
instead of ticket holders/

writers & arrangers/
instead of BET whores & MTV trash/
remember my brothers & sisters...that.../
you are a people of profound blackness/
& people of colors mixed with ancient spirits.../
& yes even if your soul is mixed
with a lil...white, red or yellow.../
yes did you know?/
for you see/not only does black folks ride the NYC subways system.../
this city is multi-cultural u know!/
we need everyone's help/in order to straighten' this fuckin' mess out/

& you my brother & sister/   (Man wearing orange)
want to ride a round this big ole city/
stickin' up brothers & sisters/
of all colours.../child you've been watching/
to many reruns of Gun Smoke & Rifle Man/
it' not safe.../it' just not safe.../I tell you to ride on the:

IND...inner niggers district line/   (Man wearing red)

IRT...international racist terrorist/   (Man wearing white)
or/
the.../

BMT...bigots against minorities traveling downtown/   (Man wearing beige)

&/   (Man wearing black)
all of us are wishin'/
that/E.T. would soon hurry-up & phone home/
yeah/maybe a part II movie will teach all of us/
that reaching out...means loving others & oneself/
not committing wars against the homo's/
for they are in the subway stations restroom/
serving a lot of tea/but/not getting much sympathy/
AIDS is here...it's here to stay...or at least it seems.../

yet your papa/my papa/continue to suck off trade/
from every size, shape & color/
then/go home to our mother.../

half of America/   (Man wearing purple)
is Acting-up/because/
not only are junkies & homos/
are being affected, infected or effected…
by this virus pandemic…/
yeah/we all are wonderin' how/
AIDS has now become a house hold name?/
just ask your husband/when he comes in late tonight from Grand Central
Station…/
U see/
fag bashing must stop/
black on black crime must stop/
car jacking most stop/
shooting students in public schools…/
hell/you must stop…/

VI

yes/   (Man wearing beige, while attacking the other men)
girlfriend/the words out/
that/
not only does orange bird have a break in his wing, too!/
but/
there's a whole bunch of little birdies/fallin'…/
fallin' from off of the Florida state sunshine Tropicana tree/
check out your son…/your brother…/your father…/ even your dear old husband…/
yeah/
they/maybe someone else's lover…?/
they/could have even been mine?/

hell there's a lot more going on/   (Man wearing orange)
here then just payin' the rent!/

Aretha/   (Man wearing beige)
sang: "…who's zooming who?"
hell if you don't know/i'm damn sure ain't goin' to tell you!/

Ms. Doris Day/   (Man wearing purple)
sang: "Que sera, sera"/
& look what happen to ole Rocky & Liberace/
U see their hidden diamonds…/ain't no gold, no mo'/

why?/   (Man wearing beige)
Child/I got all the dirt/while riding the "A" Train/
see/even Mr. Carl Malone doesn't care to pat Magic Johnson on his ass anymore.../

yeah, why/   (Man wearing red...while lookin' at the man wearing beige)
not phone home E.T./
for mo' freaks to honor us with their presence.../
we could all use another outlet for negative/
hostile remarks & reactions/
news from the headlines of the NY Times/the Daily News/
& yes even the tired ole NY Post/news about those freaks/
getting on & off at West 4th Street in Greenwich Village/
yeah/   (Man wearing black, looking in shock at man wearing red)
those freaks/
you're laughin' at.../maybe someone else's joy.../
perhaps even yours...oh! didn't you know?/

please/   (Man wearing red)
just a few more stations/
before/my stop & this is NYC in transit/
watch the closing/watch/watch the closing doooooooooooors.../
watch the closing doooooooooooors.../
& then/there' the madness out there on the city streets.../
hell/I just love New York.../

                    (All in unison, as they all dash off stage screamin'...
        while addressin' the audience...while throwing change at the women just to keep her quite.)

Don't you?.../

(   )

                (Enter men wearing black, red, white & blue...Man in black starts to speaks first)

just yesterday morning/while walking through morningside park/
from 7th Avenue/there were two white women.../two young white women/

now I may be generalizing here/   (Man wearing red)
but/they were cleanin'/one of those parks statues/
(you know the one with the bear/
& the young child/half beast is hiding from the bear in a cave)/
they/the two women...(please try to keep up with me...)/

they/both were most likely workin' from funds/
of $100,000.00 by the Ford Foundation/
or/on a $80,000.00 Carniegn Foundation grant/

yet/   (Man wearing blue)
within a few minutes/as I climbed the stair to the Upper Westside/
from Haarlem/there were three black women.../three young black women/
one sister was smokin' a blunt/one sister was holdin' a brown paper bag up/
to her lips & the other sister was just sittin' there...in a daze/

no/   (Man wearing white)
I am not generalizing here/for I have smoke a few blunts/
to know the smell of a blunt cigar/
& yes I have held a number of brown paper bags up to my lips/
in order to quench my thirst/& I have been in a daze my entire life.../
so I know.../

now/   (Man wearing black)
one can blame racism/the economy/
the threat of rent-control becoming non-existing/sexism/
mis-education/welfare reform/reverse affirmation actions/
& yes even slavery/but/this is 1997 not 1797 or 1897/
has some of my people forgotten the struggle?/

hell it was only 10:00 a.m./   (Man wearing red)
I just don't know.../I just don't know.../I just don't know.../

like the time/   (Man wearing white)
I saw one of my young brothers walking his pit bull/
& the pit bull was carry an NBA basketball.../
an NBA basketball/I kid u not...a NBA basketball.../
now see I could understand/if it was a got damn chicken bone.../

but an NBA basketball in the dogs mouth?/   (Man wearing black)
is this some form of black manhood/
that/I had missed out on or something?/
since i'm not part of the X-Generation?/
I just don't know.../I just don't know.../I just don't know...

this morning/   (Man wearing red)
while walking home from the Upper Westside to Haarlem/
& yes, I'm spellin' H-A-A-R-L-E-M with 2 "aa's since I've

learned that the Dutch spelled it this way in the 1600s-since my teachers never did/
yo, wait...
I saw two brothers just sittin' on the park bench/
once again in daze/& then I'd notice in Samuel Maxx Park/
that two Asian-Americas sittin' in the blazing sun...among cracks head/
wearing high heels and tube socks...(no, no, not the Asian-Americans/
not the two crack heads...will you please try to keep up...)/

while/   (Man wearing white)
walking towards the A. Philip Randolph housing complex/
there were a horde of my people/just sitting & enjoyin' the summer breeze/
yet i wonder how many of them know who A. Philip Randolph is? Or was?/

yeah just the other day/   (Man wearing black)
while/walkin' toward the #2 train station at 110th Street & Lenox.../
three lil black boys/stop me & asked: "Mr. *do you have a 25c...*"/
hell it was 9:00 a.m./on a school day?
(& yes I gave them each a $ a piece.../
only because adult' were kind to me...in my youth...)/

yeah/   (Man wearing red)
I have been in a daze my entire life/
I just don't know.../I just don't know.../I just don't know.../

we are only three years short/   (Man wearing black shakes his head...they all exit)
of the year 2000/
have we forgotten the struggle/
I just don't know.../I just don't know.../I just don't know.../I just don't know...

(This poem can be omitted for brevity...)

(Enters men wearing beige, purple & orange/Man wearing purple starts to speak)

I can read a queen on any hot day of the week/
down by the piers/
but/what can one do when your late for work/
& the boss man never let' you forget it?/

but/   (Man wearing beige)
i'm trying to be as/discrete as possible/
when a piece I picked up late last night from Keller's Bar/
or was it early this morning/left me/

after our submission of heated passion & lust/
which/I thought was love/love that subsided.../& love no, no, no/
not love/but pure unadulterate sex/raw & hard core butt fuckin'.../

his words exactly: (Man wearing beige addresses the audience)

"...baby, this can only happen.../   (Man wearing orange)
this can only happen just this once.../
see I have to get home to my wife & kids..."/

damn it/   (Man wearing beige)
just for once/
I would like to forget about acting discrete/
& instead of reading my brothers down by the piers/
love them with kindness & understandin'/
understandin'/that we're all in this whirlpool of misery loves company/
in this whirlpool of misery loves company...together!/

day by day/   (Man wearing purple)
a gathering of stranger/out of a mutual bond of loneliness.../
from a livin' a life of conditional love.../

&/   (Man wearing beige)
when the boss man/
bitches.../
I shall pull out my tally sheets of overtime/
special assignments & long meetings/
while being held over thru lunch/that I've never completed
'cause/as the boss man stated a number of times:

"...you're the best man for the job/   (Man wearing orange)
& you're single too!" no responsibilities my ass!"/

being single is a state/   (Man wearing purple)
of responsibilities if only to oneself/

you see the double-life I live/   (Man wearing beige)
from Wall Street Executive to Christopher Street whore/
it's as hard as sucking a bull' tit for milk/
yet, i'm trying to be as discrete...discrete as possible/
as I continue to meet/& greet the boys down by the piers off of Christopher St./
& as I long for some peace & company/

if just for a little while/before going back/
to Wall St. & the boss man…

                    (All the men embrace/then they exit/except man wearing beige)

(   )

                (Enters men wearing brown & green/Man wearing brown starts to speak)

just one day/
I would like/
to stop someone & talk without any misgiving' nor pretenses/

poet: "…oh, excuse me mister can…I…"   *(Man wearing beige)*

man: "…can you what?…mother fucker! I'll blow your
brains out! Are you queer or something?"   *(Man wearing green)*

Like the song says: *(Man wearing brown)*

"…ain't no stopping us now   *(Man wearing beige)*
were on the move…"
(to where/would somebody please tell me?)

"I know some people that have a negative vibe…"
(Family/friends/co-workers/politicians & the average joe blow from off of the city streets)

all of them are narrow minded/   *(Man wearing brown)*

"but where they end up, I don't know…"   *(Man wearing beige
                                           when the woman enters)*

poet: "…excuse me miss, but I would like to just express my feelings
           about the…way you look this beautiful morning."

woman: "…why thank you my brotha…"   *(Woman speaks)*

poet: "…may I walk with you a lil bit?   *(Man wearing beige)*
           I just want to share some ideas
           & my social opinions with someone…"

woman: "Sure, but first let's get one thing Straight…"   *(Woman speaks)*
             (No pun intended, i'm sure)
             "…It's going to cost you $50.00 bucks

& then we can get high & talk until your time is up..."

poet: "I might as well continue writing on..."   (Man wearing beige)

but/   (Man wearing brown)
just one day/
I would like to stop someone & talk without any misgiving' nor pretenses

            (Man wearing beige is running after both men & the woman as they exits)

"...oh
excuse me can I..."

(This poem can be omitted for brevity...)

there's a ship/   (Man wearing purple)
due to come my way/& the captain/
& crew will be dressed to kill/& like some rat/
you would have left many days before/but/
there's a ship due to come my way/
where i'll be held hostage/to live out their's & my wildest fantasy.../

foolish you say?   (Man wearing purple addresses the audience...)

but/there's a ship due to come my way/where/there'll be jewels & golden harps.../
harp' playin' sweet chamber music.../

                (Enters man wearing beige then addresses the audience...)

music fit for this queen of the night/
wishful thinking you say/I know.../I know.../I know.../
but/this is my fairy tale/
& like all fairies/

                (Looks over at the man wearing beige...who exits stage left)

i'll dream of ships/& rugged crew members/
jewels & golden harps playin' sweet chambers music.../
music...fit for any queen.../fit for any queen of the night/
yes/I can see it now/for there's/
a ship/
due to come my way.../   (Man wearing purple runs off after man wearing beige)

(　　　)

(Enters men wearing red, black & blue...man wearing black speak first)

I

I was only a child during the '60s/nobody taught me about/
The "King"/"Malcolm X" nor the "Kennedy's" of that time.../&

now that i'm apart of that same GeNeRaTiOn/   (Man wearing blue)
that/they tried to teach & protect so well/that/
it cost them their lives (AnD I SaY)/Jesus (AiN't ThE oNlY oNe)/
who die for my sins/&

(Enters man wearing beige...)

I wOnDeR/ShOuLd I Be GrAtEfUl   (All the men say this in unison)

i've listen 2 the old QuEeNs/   (Man wearing beige)
from the KnIgHts at the RoUnDtAbLeS bar in Greenwich Village/
& the ones at
& 43rd St. BlUeS bar/but/the young ones at KeLlEr's bar/
don't want to.../it's all about them wantin' muscle 2.../
Yes/it's so sad/that Michael Jackson had to let Ms. Ross sing his song.../

one day Michael/
one day you wouldn't have to sing, "Billie Jean' not my lover..."/&

I wOnDeR/ShOuLd I Be GrAtEfUl   (All the men In unison...)

listening to their talks/those ole QuEeNs in those gay bars...talkin'/
of StOnEwAlL RiOts in the late 60s/& loving everyone/
from Sly & the Family Stone 2 Snow White/
(Get Black Jack, that wasn't for us in the 70s nor 80s...)/
all because/half of some Black/gay/men mental concept of Unity/
during the 80s expanded no further then the TrAdE sittin' next to them.../
& havin' them think of 69 different ways of having fair trade exchange/
that same day/that same nite:
"only if he's big & don't turn over"—you know that's right girl...(with a SNAP!!!)

II

& we all know about that don't we?/cat's got your tongue?/better the got damn cat/
than some ass hole/remember no funding nor ACT-UP marches/
by black gay men...yet for A.I.D.S. research/

it's only a WhItE cReAmYDiSeAsE.../   *(Man wearing red)*

         (Man wearing black...everyone else is in shock that he use the "N" word fully...)

N-I-G-G-E-R!!!! don't U read the newspapers?/

...look at what happened to/   *(Man wearing blue)*
Vanessa Williams...still our Ms. America/
now, America/is welcome to Ms. William's "Comfort Zone"/
(Penthouse, remember ain't nothing like sweet revenge/sweet revenge)
& Rev. Jesse Jackson/our only backbone politician (then again may be not).../
hell we waited for over 300 plus 4 years/what's another 4 mo'/

oh! there's much mo'/   *(Man wearing beige)*
but later.../&

I wOnDeR/ShOuLd I Be GrAtEfUl   *(All the men In unison)*

III

...damn it took decades/   *(Man wearing black)*
4 me 2 have been allowed to sit next 2 a white man/
& drink a glass of water/read the Daily News/
while we both took a shit in public toilets.../

& now years later/   *(Man wearing beige)*
i've learned to sit/eat/laugh & turn the other cheek/or/
shall I say...spread the other cheeks.../
in order to give them an example of my sexual being.../
while taking pride in my fellowman/&
then being asked to go home with him & I say bullshit.../

who's shit?/   *(All the men in unison)*

it's getting hot & funky/   *(Man wearing beige)*
(yeah I'm about to set it off up in here)/&

I wOnDeR/ShOuLd I Be GrAtEfUl   (All the men In unison...)

4 not knowing my blackness 1st/   (Man wearing beige)
& my sexual livelihood 2nd/while/
my beautiful black/latino sisters & brothers/
"R" still waitin' on some relief line for some handout programs/
since 1984/or/waitin' for this & not getting much of that!/

while i'm/   (Man wearing blue)
wined & dined & treated 2 erotic cities:

Paris, Brussels, Holland & Rome.../   (Man wearing black)

all/   (Man wearing red)
because of my sexual strength.../&
it doesn't matter/
whether I am or am not called a sybarite/
& accustomed to such things or not...or if it's all just a media myth/
when it comes to the size of my dick.../& I say again.../
hell...my white counterparts.../they don't care...nor do some of my brother'.../

&/I say Bullshit/who's shit again.../   (Man wearing beige)

        (Man wearing beige addresses the audience & then the other men)

& I say to my people/love & respect me 4 what I am/
& more likely to become.../just a black man who love' other men/
& a black man who respect & loves my black women, too!/
perhaps/then U 2 can share in the colorful/
& carefree life I've chosen 2 live/but/only on the weekends/
cause I pay my dues on my 9 to 5/just like all the rest of Ussssss.../
then/perhaps the next generations wouldn't have 2/
wonder should they/
be or not be GrAtEfUl...   (All the men exits from various volms...on stage)

(   )

I am the product of: (Enters man wearing black)

the civil rights era/the BEATLES/the SUPREMES/both the KOREAN/
& VIETNAM wars/the 1963 march on Washington/the first man to walk on the moon/
the KENNEDY klan/MEDGER W EVERS/DR M. L. KING, Jr.,/
& a brother named MALCOLM/a brother who replaced his slave name/

to El-Hajj Malik El-Shabazz & his outlook on life/which caused so much confusion/
that had some settling for camping out at WOODSTOCK/
while singin' & gettin' high/& sunbathin' in the nude/LSD trippin'/
rather than thinkin' about the killin' of a black PRINCE & KING/
& other noble men of color.../
Not to mention/the battle' at KENT STATE & ATTICA STATE PRISON.../
battle' that caused the death of innocent: students, sons, brothers & fathers.../&

I am the product of: (Enters man wearing beige)

musicals called HAIR/& the *AGE of AQUARIUS*/
& the Oscar going to LIZA M. instead of DIANA R./
& now we know why the *LADY SANG THE BLUES*.../
or why Sister Tyson opted to married Bro. Miles & create her very on "Sound...er"/
boycotts against Woolworths/LSD trippin'/& ridin' white ladies/
while callin' their mother SMACK/bein' called a FLOWER CHILD/
the ERA movement & the burnin' of 16-hour Bras/the Watergate Scandal/

sister NINA SIMONE singin' "MISSISSIPPI GODDAMN"/
then/watchin' her & brother JAMES "JIMMY" ARTHUR (JONES) BALDWIN/
dash off to EUROPE/
in order to seek creative freedom/only to find refuge in "Giovanni's Room"/
sister ANGELA Y. DAVIS & sister NIKKI GIOVANNI/
two sisters lovin' brothers/while/
still talkin' about guns & startin' revolutions/
& bein' two total black women at the same time.../
while givin' birth to a new GeNeRaTiOn/
& sister JoAnne Chesimard/
runnin' from bein' a target of J. EDGAR HOOVER legacy/
& the NJ State Troopers biases actions.../

which tried to:
"...defame, infiltrate & criminalize me..."   (Spoken by the woman...)

her words, not mine/   (Man wearing beige, addresses the audience...)
that/
caused her to change her name to Assata Shakur & seek Castro's help in Cuba/
(but lets not forget Castro's selling of Cuban 17 year old boys.../
uhm, for God only know?)/
Perhaps, we should have asked Reinaldo Arenas?
oh, yes/let' not forget about Patty Hearst/
& her Oscar performance or was it her daddy's money?/&

I am the product of: (Enters man wearing blue)

"*Please...Please...Please...,*" Mr. Postman/
brin' MAMA her 1st & 2nd welfare check/on the 1st & 16th of every month/
4 U see/the LANDLORD is knocking at the front door/
while BIG DADDY waltzes out of the back door/BIG DADDY finally realized/
that he was no longer MAMAs sweet meat.../MAMA/did what she had to do/
she was young/uneducated & BLACK & she had ten lil mouth' to feed/
the LANDLORD/the LANDLORD/u see didn't have to knock anymo'/
cause he used his very own KEY.../&

I am the product of: (Man wearing beige)

JEAN CARNs singin' "*Free love*"/SYLVESTER makin' everyone "*Feel Mighty Real*"/& I was
with DIANA ROSS/when she had her "*Love Hangover*"/
as I became envious of GLORIA GAYNOR/
as she chanted, "*I Will Survive...*"/all the way to the bank/
is it true? that DONNA SUMMER rode the coat tails of the Gay communities/
then turned her back on them when AIDS reared it' ugly head/
saying something along the lines, that her "*God*" told her to do so.../
now, Donna who loves to love you baby?/&

I am the product of: (Enters man wearing red)

the death of Michael Stewart/a inner city youth/
who's blood was spilled along the corridors of NYC police station.../
for being an graphic artist/yet Keith Harring/
became an icon at Andy Walhol's Foundation for the Visual Arts, Inc.,/&

I am the product of: (Man wearing beige)

freein' myself from polyester suits/& donnin' on wigs/
&/
high heels/   (Man wearing beige starts looking around for those heels again!)
&/
false eyelashes in order to get into Studio 54/
&/
the Paradise Garage/way before there was a Boy George & Culture Club/
once again trippin' off of:
ACID, ANGEL DUST & COCAINE/while GRACE JONES sang:
"*I NEED A MAN*" & "*LA VIE EN ROSE*"
& "*PULL UP TO MY BUMPER.*" all in one breathe.../

while Tina Turner sang, "PRIVATE DANCER,"/
leavin' Ike to wallow in a state of sadness & regrets/
while he' listenin' to "*What's Love Got's To Do With It...
Got' To Do...Got' To Do With It...*"/&

I am the product of: (Enters man wearing white)

computer technology/collectin' garbage & storin' garbage.../
puttin' out nothin' but trash/ (for you see—racism found it' way on to The Internet)/
& yes i've seen the 1st Ms. Black America dethroned/
& the 3rd Black Presidential potential/talks of divestment in South Africa/
talks of freein', freein' Mandela/&

I am the product of: (Enters man wearing purple)

the future MOONWALKER/the CHALLENGER/REAGANOMICS/
NANCY & ALL OF HER STARS/
the Wall Street Money Makers & the Savin' & Loans scandal.../
the evolution of:
disco, breakdancin', rappin' to voguin' & gangster rap...
to Central Park becomin' a war zone/to Philly's Brownville bein' a war zone/&

I am the product of: (Enters man wearing brown)

crack/coke/Pepsi/estacy joy & pain/
the term yuppies/vcr-pac-a-man catch-him if you can.../
I want my MTV/& now that there's 2/4 the price of 1/
u see 4 whites MTV/& blacks/Yo! MTV Raps/
yeah, music is crossin' over/yet MTV/
remains segregated...that' why there' BET
yes, sir...yes, ma' racism is still alive & visible.../
u see/Brother James Brown went straight to jail.../&
he did not pass go.../he did not collect is $200/
yet, I'll bet you.../
yeah, I'll bet you, that if it were "*old blue eyes*" Sinatra.../
yeah, if it were "*old blue eyes*".../
The Godfather of Soul James Brown now knows/
what livin' in America is all about...from the inside/out/
unfortunately he couldn't have it his way.../&

I am the product of: (Man wearing beige)

the lines at the employment offices getting longer/
& our paychecks gettin' shorter/
AIDS survivors/findin' sympathy only through the wearin' of red ribbons.../
& walk-a-thon'/& Ryan White takin' America' old bleedin' hearts to his young grave/
i've seen China demand democracy/& the Berlin wall come tumblin' down/
while joinin' the east & west/
& the possibility of a second Presidential Impeachment.../
yes i've seen Elton John/ease the world's pain with one song/
twice...for two grand ladies/who' lives shall forever/
continue to burn like..."candles in the wind".../
Yes/all of this/all of this/as I've became a product of the last 4 decades/
all of this/all of this/
as I try to understand the past/in order to deal with the present/
while remainin' optimist about my future.../

(All the men start falling to the ground...dead or dying, except the man wearing beige
some of the men are walking with canes, some are being carried...
While Man wearing beige starts wrapping the dead bodies in white sheets...)

40 years.../
40 years.../
40 years.../
&/
not one mentionin' of my brothers/
&/
or lovers lovin' or being loved by others men
as I slowly read their obituaries.../
realizin' that I am also a product of denial.../   (Lights flash out)

(   )

(Enter man wearing black who joins man wearing beige. Man wearing black starts to speak...
while a photo of James Baldwin is showing on a background hugh screen. The remaining cast
members are wearing mask resembling, Mr. James "Jimmy" Baldwin...
Man wearing black is calling out "Jimmy, Jimmy, Jimmy!," before speaking...)

news had reached the villagers of Zimbabwe/
they called upon the n'angas.../
who were up in the high density suburbia/
as they all stood-up out of respect/

the people of Nigeria/ (Man wearing beige)
who had suffered from river blindness.../
saw his words speaking to them/about their people lives across the waters.../

there was nothing/ (Man wearing black)
nothing/but standing room only/
at *The Cathedral Church of St. John the Divine in Haarlem, USA*/

you see everyone/ (Man wearing beige)
else had already fallen to their knees in prayer/

there was nothing/ (Man wearing black)
nothing/yet everyone felt the intensed heat of the cities streets/
& the coolness of the day/

as/ (Man wearing beige)
people of all races/
joined in under one a chord of:
"Dear Lord, Dear Lord, why him..." (In unison...)

there was nothing/ nothing/yet/
everyone claimed to be in good spirits

which/ (Man wearing black)
shows you what great actor's mankind can truly be.../

there was nothing/ (Man wearing beige)
nothing/yet everyone praised his literary work/
his unmatched mind/his raging spirit/
his love of his people & his adoptive country/

(Man wearing black speak while the woman dress in black slowly walks cross the stage...)

all the mourners/praised their/
Buddha, Allah, Rabbi, Yahway, Jehovah & even Jesus Christ, etc., etc.../

there was nothing/ (Man wearing beige)
nothing/yet everyone turned towards him/
awaiting for a miracle to happen.../

yes/ (Man wearing black)
miracles do happen/some must stay/
while other must go away.../

as the crowd of mourners passed the open grave/
& stop to place rose petals/
you could see in the corner of everyone's eyes.../
a tiny little tear drop.../

while/   *(Man wearing beige, while the woman reaches*
an/   *the other side, starts singing...)*
ole woman started to hum "Go Tell It On The Mountain."

         (Both men run to the woman & joins her in a chorus of the song &
                  slowly walks off stage/Light dim down)

(This poem can be omitted for brevity...)

      (The song "Lush Life" is softly played off stage, then enters man wearing black,
        who takes on the role of a bartender, and starts setting up the bar...
            Enters man wearing white who starts to speak...)

I

I am told that on any giving night.../

      (Then Michael Stone's, original piece "Men in Smoked Filled Bars" is heard)

one can see men & even young boys roamin' through NYC Central Park/
like hungry savages/darting in & out of the city park's trees & broken branches/
near an area called "the RAMBLES..."/

I am also told/   *(Enters man wearing orange & gets a drink from the bar)*
that/
the "A" train can take one there/if one dare to go...would you?/

there was a place/   *(Enters man wearing beige...joinin' man wearing white at the bar)*
a place/
called the Nickel Bar not too far from Manhattan's mid-town crowd/
where tourist & natives alike stop for .50 hot dogs/
on the corner of 72nd Street & B'way/where NYC gay chaps/stop/
after mergin' from the no. 2 or 3 trains station/

yes/   *(Man wearing purple)*
these gay chaps were hangin' out at the Nickel Bar & 96 West/
or at Jay's & Andre's uptown in Harlem.../

talkin'/dancin'/eatin' potato chips/& sippin' imported beer (side-by-side)/
while stealin' quite glances/
yet hopin' to meet someone to make them feel loved.../
at least for that night...since they haven't learn how to do it themselves.../
& if by chance/
their eyes did meet...yes two stranger' in the night.../
these gay young chaps.../out of fear of rejection/would quickly look downward/
starin' down at images of George Washington/
& ole Georgie would be starin' back at them.../

you see/   (Man wearing beige)
at the Nickel Bar the counter tops/
were encased in glass & underneath the glass was nickels/
& used chewing gum/these were the only three things separating the gay chaps/
& the first President of this here great U.S. of A.../
nickels/beer stains/& there was also another form of separation.../
the/separation of beer stain rings/between the glass counter top/
& the nickels/uhm/aren't gay chaps so richly creative...?

II

...yes times/   (Man wearing orange)
have changed/since women were asked to dance for .10 a dance.../
back in the good ole days/today/boys who became men overnight/
danced a dual of unspoken passion/with/hopes of gettin' back in return/
a chance to spend a night with other lonely strangers.../
lonely strangers/who dared to glance long enuf/
& far enuf pass those stained nickels/between the Nickel Bars glass counter top.../
there/at the Nickel Bar/boys/men
were awaitin' their chance at heated/cheap city parks & bathroom stall romances.../
let' not forget the Ansonia Bathes/where Bette Milder & Barry Manilow & Larry Levan
once peformed for those same boys/men & their unspoken passion.../
while sitting in the sauna room/completely nude.../
yet still pretending no one can see them.../

yes/   (Man wearing beige)
can we speak freely for a moment or too!/...about.../
about life in general/I mean about hot burning passions/
injustice/women/gays/people of color/
& when do we draw the line on labeling? & the passin' of judgement?/

labels concernin'/ (Man wearing white)
what' right & what' wrong.../
hey I am asking you?/yes you?
don't be alarmed!/ (Man wearing white is addressing the cast & audience)
hey don't even be ashamed!/
it' just plain talk among misty smoke filled bars.../
while I just sit here with a couple of gay chaps/
chit-chatting, sippin' beer...just for the hell of it!/

let' make it everyone'/ (Man wearing beige)
business to know...the real deal here/
A.I.D.S is here/& it looks as if it will be here for awhile.../
thank' to the denial of A.I.D.S. existence/by the White House...
under Reagan Administration in the early 80s/
& the NY Times, December 7th, 1987 article stating/
that/the Black/Latino communities are at high risk.../
& those lonely souls just kept right on sippin' imported beers/
& watered down rum & coke/livin' the "Lush Life"/
straight out from a Billy Strayhorn' song/
while some of us were dyin' from denial.../

some folks/ (Man wearing orange)
thought everything was going to be alright/
as long as A.I.D.S./stayed in the gays/homos/junkies/Haitians/
& tinted blood victims very own got damn backyards!/

it' a shame/ (Man wearing purple)
that America'/
figured it was "those" other people problem/
& not the holy than thou bible belts/pray snatchers...problem too!/
until we lost two of Americans heroes.../
yes the Pajama games are over for Rock Hudson & Liberace/
who left us all with a spellbound existin' concerto no. 5/

(Man wearing beige...while watching some of the men walking with canes
& others holding each other up for support)

you see A.I.D.S. finally made it' way uptown/
even 125th in Haarlem has a place where "those" special people all meet.../
called the Mt. Morris Bathes & child it' no YMCA/
it' been there for over 90 some odd years! (without renovation)/

III

now I am told/   (Man wearing white)
just before A.I.D.S. made it' way uptown/
it stop at the Nickel Bar on 72nd Street midtown/

just two blocks/   (Man wearing purple)
away from the most famous & talked about tourist park.../

i'm also told/   (Man wearing white)
while chattin' in those smoked filled misty bars/
that/in the late 70s the Nickel Bar/was very hot, hot, hot...actual real hot!/

then/   (Man wearing beige)
came the 80s/& the boys who became men overnight/
was forced to cool down/if not cool off completely/& a few damn near chilled the
fuck right on out.../

long before/   (Man wearing orange)
Ms. Jennifer Levin met her untimely fate/yes by the hands of Mr. Robert Chambers.../
the young woman was killed in the city park while engagin' in a sexual liaison/
we all had wished/   (Man wearing purple)
for the nightmare to end/   ,
because while Mr. Chambers was copin' a deadly feel/

there were/   (Man wearing beige)
men & young boys/lurkin' among those same trees & branches/
seeking the same pleasure.../doing the same thing/playin' with danger.../
the same men & young boys/who continued to come out way past midnight.../
looking for unspoken passion in terms of love from dusk til dawn.../

IV

I remember: (Man wearing white)
Roberta Flack & Donny Hathaway singin' of
"being back together again"/
& so did the gay chaps in those smoked filled bars.../
until their bartender Louie died so mysteriously/

Ms. Ross sang/   (Man wearing beige)
about "coming out"/

but around 1985 or was it 1986 A.I.D.S. was becomin' a household name/
& some of us was thinkin' of returnin' to the ole faithful closet/
realizin' once again/
that/a backlash of Stonewall/
& the eve of Judy Garland' death…that this illness/
which was killing so many of us…was a serious health issue/and could not be ignored/
Yoko Ono (Lennon's widow)/
sang of "*walking on thin ice*"/
& the gay chaps in these smokey filled midst bars/
were wonderin' how could she tell…?/

& not being able to foreseeeeeein'/   (Man wearing purple)
John bein' gun down/
while those same men & boys were "*walking on thin ice*"/
& leavin' or enterin' the 72nd Street/
& the 81st Street entrances of Central Park West/
among the crowds of Beatles fans & NYC finest/
after just feedin' themselves upon unspoken passion/
& a piece of a lil night' action/

the night/   (Man wearing beige)
John Lennon was killed…/
the boyz/men were partakin' in their own death'/
John's death should have warned us all…/
that/the "*children of the night*" /the same children/that the Jones Girls sang about/
needed to "*come together right now…*"/

yet/   (Man wearing purple & beige dances…
the boys/   while man wearing white starts talking…)
who became men overnight/
walked pass the scene of John's murder/
on the eve of that historical night' event/
the boys/
who became men overnight/
they walked along 72nd Street with there heads among the clouds & stars/
headin' right towards the Nickel Bar/& continued to dance a macabre (pas de deux)/
until some of them started to drop one-by-one/out of sight…/out of sight/
right into a sea of denial…/

(Man wearing oranges starts to sing while the two men are still dancing…)

"imagine there' no heaven/it's easy if you try…"

since life for some is a living hell/it' believable/
if what was once a man's almond joy in the late night hours/
can now become his livin' hell in the morning time/

in the mid 80s/   (Man wearing white)
Dear Death: sat himself down right at the entrance doors/
of not only the Nickel Bar/but/the Paradise Garage/96 West/
Better Day, & even Keller'/takin' head count of those who did not make it back/
from the parks/bathes the nights before…/

        (Man wearing purple pushing away from man wearing beige/The music stops…
                    man wearing beige starts to speak…)

you see A.I.D.S. isn't colored blind/
nor sexist…/it closed the 72nd street Nickel Bar in mid-town/
where the gay chaps at the those smoked filled misty bars/
were hangin' out way pass midnight…/
some of them dyin'…/some of them survivin'…/
some of them in a state of denial/like I said:
some of them dyin' from havin' been served not much tea/
but/a hell of a lot of unspoken passion & half-ass sympathy…

        (Each man grabs one another as the lights fade out…a moment of silences)

(   )

        (Enters men wearing brown, red & black…man wearing brown speaks.)

the surgeon general & even a few hollywood stars & the first lady/
are now my so called role models/

they/   (Man wearing red)
all seem to be on the ban wagon…/
the ban wagon for America to just say no/

say no to drugs/   (Man wearing black)
say no to sex/& even rap/
hip hop & yes good ole rock & roll music/

yet/   (Man wearing brown)
they offer us no alternatives…/
except a cheap slogan/a slogan/that simply states: practices safe sex!/

yet/   (Man wearing red)
we don't practice/
what we all know some of us are preachin'.../

for what we don't/   (Man wearing black)
teach at home we damn sure don't want someone else/
to teach us in our schools either!/
sought of a catch 22/damn if you do & damn if you don't/
sought of situation wouldn't you say?/

the whores on the city streets/   (Man wearing brown)
they don't listen.../

the boys/men/   (Man wearing red)
on their knees in most city parks/after the sun goes down/
they don't listen.../

the young mother's/   (Man wearing black)
who has yet another mouth to fed/
& her very own homework to do/it's obvious she didn't listen.../

the cocaine user/   (Man wearing brown)
the crack heads/
the wall street executive/
the swinging couples on their neighbors water beds.../
who's becomin' well known on the Internet for practicin' 69 different positions/
in a one night stand/
they for sure aren't listenin'.../

the friends/   (Man wearing red)
both gay/straight/bi/transgender/or what-have-you/
black/white/Asian/& other people of color/
rich/poor/famous/& the not so famous/to the unknown & all of the above.../
who are droppin' like flies.../it's evident they didn't listen/
or/if they did/it was to late.../

but/   (Man wearing black)
i'm no fool to realize/
that/j.o. is the best alternative.../
hey/let's all practice what we are preachin'/
& while we're at it/please pass the Kleenex...

(*A box of Kleenex is throw from off stages,*
all the man run off the opposite directions laughing...)

(This poem can be omitted for brevity...)

(Enters men wearing white, blue & green/Man wearing white starts to speaks)

how soon we tend to forget/
the days of our youth.../

&/   *(Man wearing blue)*
pencil composition/pumpkin seeds/Mary Janes/
Grape Now/Laters & Lemon Drops.../

the days/   *(Man wearing green)*
of passe' frolic.../

lil boy'/   *(Man wearing white)*
wearin' knickers & tweeded apple jacks.../

lil girl'/   *(Man wearing green)*
in bobby sox & poodle skirts.../

short hair...long hair/   *(Man wearing blue)*

marches to & fro/   *(Man wearing white)*
riots/wars/to runnin' off to Canada from being drafted.../

the age of video mania/   *(Man wearing green)*
& the Watergate tapes.../

yes, as American eases/   *(Man wearing white)*
into a pair of 501s.../

neglectin'/   *(Man wearing blue)*
today' children/
who are homeless/miseducated & when seekin' refuge/
become members/
of the crips & bloods...

(All the men dashes from off stage as gun shots are being heard from off stage somewhere)

(   )

(*Enters men wearing black, orange, green & purple/Man wearing black speaks first...*)

on the streets of Brooklyn/my/wandering Jew grows.../

in the city/   (*Man wearing green*)
that never sleeps/my wandering Jew thirsts/
for a drink of compassion/

in Christian homes/   (*Man wearing purple*)
right next to their book of litany/
my wandering Jew feels safe & secure in Christian churches/
right next to St. Jude rest my wandering Jew/

in Baptists homes/   (*Man wearing orange*)
right along side the Holy Bible/
& half eaten peach cobbler & newly baked banana bread/
my wandering Jew becomes spiritually fed.../

in Baptist churches/   (*Man wearing purple*)
my wandering Jew sat among Sister So & So/
& all the brothers & deacons, too!/as they all gather to sing *"Amazing Grace..."*/
rememberin' it use to be one of mama' favorite songs.../

in Muslim homes/   (*Man wearing green*)
my wandering Jew is placed very carefully next their Holy Koran/
& reads quietly *"How to Eat To Live"*/

in Muslims Mosques/   (*Man wearing black*)
where often rhetoric of Malcolm X & Muhammad Speaks/
is often heard discussed among my wandering Jew.../

see...my/   (*Man wearing orange*)
wandering Jew came to being/even way before Ellis Island/
opened its gates to immigrants from aboard.../

my/   (*Man wearing green*)
Nam-yo-ho-rengo-kyo brothers & sisters/
may have placed my wandering Jew on their Buddhist alters/
along the side of some C-Town' fresh fruits/
& burning candles/
& scents from sandalwood/while chantin' away negative karma/
& praying for world peace/

for...my wandering Jew   (Man wearing black)
outstretches its spider-like leaves/
while surroundin' my outstretched hands as I lift them.../
their spider-like leaves resembles snowy & white-stripped foliage/

my wandering Jew/   (Man wearing orange)
has a long history of sufferin'.../

see...legend has it/   (Man wearing purple)
that Christ condemned them/
to wander the earth until Christ's second coming.../

well/   (Man wearing black walks off with the plant as lights fade out)
until then/
I am just going to continue to water them/
& give it lots of love & sunlight right here on my block in Brooklyn.../

(   )

            (Enters men wearing white, beige & brown...man wearing white speaks)

everyone ought to pray/
pray to something/pray to someone for every & anything.../

see/   (Man wearing brown)
all I have to do/
is hold up my outstretched hands/
toward the heaven' above/
then/
wait for a shower of blessin' to come pourin' down from whatever God'/
might hear my prays.../

my/   (Man wearing white)
heart is so filled/
that/at times it seems.../it may have never been empty.../

my burdens were so heavy/   (Man wearing brown)
that/I now have a light outlook/
on what' bound to come my way.../

my sins/   (Man wearing beige)
are to many to share & to few/
that I don't think the world really gives a damn.../

(134)   BlAcKpOeMoLoGy

compared/   (Man wearing beige looks over at men wearing brown & white)
to their/
own troubles.../

so/   (Man wearing brown)
i'll just have to continue to stretch out my hands/
to the heaven' above & pray that a blessin' will soon come my way.../

my heart is filled with emptiness.../   (Man wearing white)
my burdens are so heavy/
heavy from sins too many to share/with anyone/
except to God's listenin' ear/in the heaven' above...

(   )

        (Enters men wearing blue, yellow, orange & beige man wearing blue starts to talk)

some go through life/like a queen sitting/upon her golden throne/

some go through life/   (Man wearing beige)
content on being a queen/ without a throne/

some go through life/   (Man wearing yellow)
like a horse tied to a stagecoach/

some go through like/   (Man wearing orange)
like a wild stallion/never knowin' the touch of a leather saddle/
forever allowin' the desert winds/to ride upon its bare back

some go through life/   (Man wearing blue)
sippin' tea from a cup & saucer/
while/others/have died in the Boston harbor/
ironic/
but/
true/
one would think/that/high taxes on tea/is a high price to pay/
for/a human life...yet/

some go through life   (Man wearing white)
oversteppin' some brother/
down on his luck/
holdin' on for dear life/strivin' to pick himself up/from the gutter/

some go through life/   *(Man wearing beige)*
dinin' on pheasant under a glass/
& sippin' dom perrigon

some go through life/   *(Man wearing orange)*
waitin' on those who leave scraps/
from the plucked bird & drippin' of flat champagne/

some go through life/   *(Man wearing beige)*
goin' mad from bein' caught up in the madness/
in their very own homes/causin'/them/to/give up/& take refuge in the bitter & cold earth/
& other' became madder than a mad hatter/because/they were to scared God/
wouldn't forgive them for committin' such a sin/
some go through life/   *(Man wearing white)*
with/their pockets filled with coins/

while/   *(Man wearing blue)*
some go through life/with their pockets filled with lies/
cause they may have only a dime or two to their name/

then/   *(Man wearing beige)*
there/are those who have never been/
given life/or/once given life/had/to be hunted down like some dog/
& then/there/are those/yet to come/
& so/the cycle will soon repeat itself/again/again/
& again/

like/   *(All in unison, before running off stage…)*
we/were sayin'/some go through life/
as if there are holes in their souls…

(   )

I found it to be true/   *(Enters man wearing red speaking)*
that life is for the living…/
that life is for the dying & in between…nothing else really matters!/
I found it to be true/that fire is like ice/ice is like fire…/
see/they both can burn you…/hey didn't you know?/I found it to be true/
that after one learns all of his & her ABC's/he or she must start all over again…/
see living is learning/learning is living/living is learning/
yes life does repeat itself…I do believe…/
I found it to be true/that folks forever are wonderin'/

which came first/the got damn chicken or the motherfuckin' egg.../
who's on first & who's on second & who didn't get a chance to past GO/
yet, instead went straight to JAIL.../
see havin' a monopoly on one's life is like a livin' hell/
& then you die!/I found it to be true/
that if one is too end up incarcerated/incarcerated...with...chains around their minds/
incarcerated...by having chains around their minds/
incarcerated...in keeping chains around their minds.../
do so/in order for the law makers & power shakers of the world.../
to continue to sip champagne.../sip champagne from their crystal glassware/
while living in their glass house'.../yet before I died & go straight to hell/
will someone please give me a couple of stones to toss along the way...

(Man wearing red exits...)

(   )

(Enters men wearing black, yellow, beige & red...black speak first)

all I know about life/is that you live/then you die!/

all I know about life /   (Man wearing yellow)
is that faith mends the lame/
& heals the sick/
& have mercy on one' sinful soul/comforts the lonely/
& is strong enuf...strong enuf to engulf a crowd/
while enablin' proud men to become humble men.../

all I know about life/   (Man wearing black)
I've learned from year' of trial & error/
year' of havin' my fare share of joy & pain/

all I know about life/   (Man wearing red)
I've seen from the dark end of life' tunnel/
where there was supposed to have been/
just a speck of light until one's death.../

all I know about life/   (Man wearing beige)
I've read about only in fairytales.../
fairytales/that/(for me) never once came true.../
see, I've giving up playing make believe.../
thinking one day some honey would kiss this here toad/

& turn me into a prince among men.../see, i've grown wise from/
just sitting among other toads/here on a lily pond...(cribbet, cribbet, cribbet)/

all I know about life/   (Man wearing red)
I've seen from a crack/a crack from dirty window panes/
window panes/that look over vacant lots/where as a child/
I'd played among bullet shells & crack vales & needles/
that pointed for some/toward an nothin' less destiny.../

all I know about life/   (Man wearing black)
I've smelled from a dash of Palmolive & a sprinkle
of all temperature Cheer...the same stuff mama used to cleanse/
cleanse the stanch from the soaked/
virgin' blood garments/
from mama' mama slave master rapacious ways.../

all I know about life/   (Man wearing beige)
i've learned from life' school of bumps & bruises/
& that sometimes one maybe flyin' high in the month of May/
only to be cut down in the month of June.../
i've also learned from livin' this here life...is...that sometimes/
is...that...sometimes one can be cut right down on the spot.../

all I know about life.../   (Man wearing yellow)
I found out from learnin'/
to pick myself up from off the ground/
& by keepin' my chin up/although my head may have well been hangin' down.../
yet managin' to place my feet on solid ground/
with both of my hands stretched upward/
searching for God's answers/
among the heavens & stars & clouds...   (All the men fall to their knees in pray...)

(   )

yes/   (Enters man wearing blue speaking as if he's giving a sermon)
I've/
agreed to come to the conclusion rather much later on...in my life.../
but/
early enuf & right on time/
that/
it would in deed.../in deed/have been a different matter/
a different choice/to say the least/to thank you, Jesus!/

yeah, some of my brother'/made a choice.../
it was too either sell their souls/
& enjoy a good roll in the hay.../
while other's made a choice/
sometimes fighting by themselves/
then/decided to turn instead toward the Holy Ghost.../
yes/it would be quite different/to just give thanks to the Lord up above.../
a choice to thank the spirit of God/
that/
moves within one's sinful soul...   (Man wearing blue join' the other men in pray)

(This poem can be omitted for brevity...)

I have ran off/   (Enter man wearing orange)
with the blazing sun.../
I have danced/
with the morning' dew/
while smilin' all the time through the pourin' down rain/
I have sat & reflected upon what direction my life has come to thus far/
I have come to realize the seriousness/
of my past travels/
which/now leads me to a state of feelin' lost/
forever/until I started countin' my blessing'/
forever/yes/is a mighty long/long time/
to promise the Lord my poor soul to keep...

            (Joins the other men in prayer...only to stop upon hearing the voice of the woman)

(   )

According to Merriam Webster Collegiate @ Dictionary: (Spoken by a woman...)

sort: to put in a certain place or rank according to kind, class, or nature; to free of confusion; to examine in order to clarify; and or to join or associate with others esp. of same kind.

sought: past or past tense of seek. <u>This Poet decided to use both forms interchangeably</u>.

                (Man wearing black stops praying to speak...
            "Ballad of The Sad Young Men" by Roberta Flack is heard from offstage...)

I sought after black men in my youth/not out of lust/
but from a remote sense of alienation/

black men were sort of a rare breed/in my little world of:
beautiful/strong/intelligent black mothers/sisters/aunts & cousins/
a world of black women/
whose laughter from the kitchen/touched upon the aroma of cinnamon/
& other spices
& of the sounds of both their joy & pain from behind closed bedroom doors/
their gossipin' on the telephones/
to distant black women.../
about their distant black men/
the same black men/
I sought after in my youth.../
I sought after black men in my youth/

(Man wearing orange stands and starts to speak)

like the sunsets & the moon rises/
only to have the sunrise all over again.../

I sort after black men in my youth/   (Man wearing red stands and starts to speak)
like a warm embrace that follows/
a gentle kiss.../oh, yes i've known of kisses/
kisses from beautiful/strong & intelligent black women.../
kisses & warm embraces from mama/grandma, sisters, aunties
& even daddy's whores.../

(Man wearing beige stands and starts to speak...cutting off man wearing red, while addressing audience)

oh, Lord forgive him.../he meant to say, "other women"

I sought after black men/   (Man wearing blue stands and starts to speak...)
like I sort after God/
for answers to my questions in my youth/
yet neither one appeared to rescue/this boy child/this boy child/this boy child.../

until years later.../   (Man wearing black)
when I learned to redefine my questioning/
& the definition of black manhood/

I sort after black men/   (Man wearing beige)
like the summer seeks autumn/autumn seeks winter & winter seeks spring/

yes I sought after black men in my youth.../   (All in unison...)

but from being a youth/ (Man wearing beige)
to now becoming a manchild myself/
& not having been held by black men in my youth/
I have now settled for being called someone else's bitch/
& at times even their whore.../while expected to scream out/yes daddy/yes daddy.../

yes I sought after black men in my youth.../black men who had not a clue as to who they were/
much less any clues as to what I was becoming.../a black man/who just wanted to be loved.../
be loved by other black men while in my youth.../

(Man wearing beige slowly embraces some men, and some resist)

until I learned to embrace black men of like minds/
& lust following desires forced reality to surface/
that the those distant black men...black men of my youth/
were men who belong not to me/but to the women of my youth...

(Once again man wearing beige starts to wrap up the falling bodies)

for I found my own black men to love & to be loved by them.../
as much as I need to be loved/
while watching them die.../while watching them die.../while watching them die.../
for the men I have found/see their death'/came to quickly & my love too late
for the men I found/stop loving & being loved.../& I pray that I continue to live...
if only for a little while.../if only for a little while, longer.../
if only for a little while longer.../if only for a little while longer.../
to love & be loved/by the black men that i've sought after.../
& as now continue to seek.../
for I've known of the love of:
beautiful/strong/intelligent black mothers/sisters/aunts & cousins.../

(Lights flashes on and off. Two bodies in sheets remain entangle on the bare staged floor...)

(   )

(Enters men wearing white, green & brown and the woman...
Man wearing green starts to speak...woman acts out role...)

an avalanche of dying spirits fell down into the valley of despair/

the villagers all felt that/ (Man wearing white)
their God's must have been angry/
for you see/their children were dying & their men were dying/
for their men were being blamed/for the death of their children/

(Man wearing brown & the woman slowly moves across the stage floor. . .)

yet/the women's wandering spirit were dying, too!/
as they continued to bury their young & their once strong men/

(Man wearing white and walks over to the woman in order to comfort her)

yet/now in their weakness they must learn to forgave them/

an avalanche of denial/   (Man wearing green)
& bitter tears fell down into the valley of despair/

the villager all felt that the God's/   (Man wearing white)
must have been angry/
to have allowed their children to die/
to have allowed their men/to carry all of the blame/
to have allow the women's spirits to wander aimlessly & ashamed/
the women chants started spreading like wildflower/

(Man wearing green is speaking over "Don't Let The Go Down On Me" by Oleta Adams)

an avalanche of broken hopes/broken dreams/broken souls/
fallen down into their valley of despair/

yet/   (Man wearing brown)
the women's wandering spirits/
continued/to bury their dead/to bury their dead & a piece of themselves

the women/   (Man wearing white)
in the valley of despair continued to chant/

(The woman starts chantin' these words. . .)

"our children are dying. . .for they all have fallen at the hands of our men's behavior"

the women's/   (Man wearing green)
chanting grew louder & louder/
until it reached: Rwanda/Haiti/Beijing/Bosnia—Herzegovina/Zaire/
& the United States of America. . .

their chanting spread like/   (Man wearing brown)
wildflower. . ./
for this illness that was killing so many innocent victims of promiscuous souls/

(All in unison...lights out...screams and moans are heard from off stage...
the woman starts singin', "Troubles of the World" softly)

was now universal & must be told.../

(This poem can be omitted for brevity...)

(Enters men wearing beige, red & blue...Man wearing beige speaks)

hello, hey yeah it's me/R U free, free as a bird U see/to talk to me/my man.../
yeah it's me/it me U see/I've been meaning to clear-up/clear-up/clear-up/
the thickness around the air that the both of us are breath' in this limited space/
of our limited existence/one calls humanity/
Yeah, it's me, it me U see attempting to clear-up some limited spacin'/
breathin' problems we two black men seems to be confronted with/
or is it only me...my brother?/we've been kicking it for sometime, now/
and I see with my bitch eyes/your family/friends don't want me around.../
for I can still call a kettle black/
& a spade a spade/
& when I'm wrong/I will swallow my mannish pride
& admit I'm wrong...yeah, my bitch eyes see all/but only tell a few things...

(Man wearing beige his talking directly to man wearing red...who ignores him.)

it's been 19 years now/   *(Man wearing blue, talking to man wearing beige...)*
19 years/
that this A.I.D.S. epidemic has been my cause & effect/
my effect & cause/my true karma/my Nam-yo-ho-rengo-ko/
my yin & yang/&yes, my Alpha/& my Omega.../my salt of the earth/
my pepper for your seasoning to match your flavor/
my holiness than thou mentality/my sinfulness/my blessed assurance/
my being damned & cursed straight to hell.../
19 years & U/me/we/& all of our other black/latino brothers...
can not see with all of "our bitch eyes..." collectively/
that/we/R, yes indeed our "Brothers Keepers"/
yes, indeed/we R/our "Brothers Keepers"/for who else will keep us/if not ourselves?/

19 years/   *(Man wearing beige talking to man wearing red,*
of me pretending/   *who's still ignoring him...)*
to being Able to your Cain/Ceaser to your Brutes/
& yes sometimes/your bitch & your whore/
yet/we both remine HIV negative/against the confusion
of this HIV positive mayhem.../

I say yes we R/   *(Man wearing blue talking to beige)*
our brother keepers/
I say yes we R/
our brother keepers/
I say yes we R/
our brother keepers/

you say/   *(Man wearing beige starts talking to man wearing red)*
we aren't/
our brother's keeper/
along with so many other brothers who R still/
sucking the life from other brothers manhood at Mt. Morris Bathhouse/
on 125th Street/24 hours/7 days a week/from 8 to 12 hours/
with one condom among them.../walking barefoot among spilled semen/
the seed of tomorrow's forgotten children.../

       (Man wearing blue is saying this to man wearing beige,who repeats it to man wearing red)

remember my brothers/
that the Ansonia Bathes on 74th B'way/was closed down in the early 80s/

19 years of our brothers/   *(Man wearing beige to man wearing blue)*
dying & Mt. Morris/
is still open.../
yes/we must be our brother's keeper/if not then who?/

we R still/   *(Man wearing blue to man wearing beige, who repeats it to)*
hanging out/
killing time/& ourselves at the N/R trains/2/3 trains/J/K trains which stops/
along the NYC/MTA Fulton Street/Court Street train station platforms/
not to mention the city parks...Rambles in Central Park West/
B'klyn' Prospect pk & St. Nicholas.../
& of coursed Riverside pk or George Michael's hanging out in Will Rogers pk/
or was it Griffin Park?

or/   *(Man wearing beige)*
Keller's Bar on the Westside Hwy./
the infamous Black male meat rack/

or dashing over/   *(Man wearing blue...)*
to Two Potato bar.../
for a hot shot of denial sexual favors.../

not one condom in sight.../invisible lives are not only in fiction novels/
but a part of yours & my reality/

19 years of this/   (Man wearing red speaks as if asking a question...)
A.I.D.S. epidemic/
19 years my brother.../

yes, I see things/   (Man wearing beige is yelling at both
with my bitch eyes/   men as they run off together...)
but only a few...of these things I care to share with U/
my beautiful blatino brother.../
& now twelve years later/I'm still wondering should I be GrAtEfUl.../
now, I realize, that by only God's grace & mercy/
i'm still here.../
i'm still here.../
i'm still here.../   (Lights fade to a spot light on man wearing beige...)

(   )

All my life/   (Man wearing beige speaks while
I've lived for a life/   "Ballad of Sad Young Man" is played...)
of contentment/peace/
& true serenity...

All my life/
thus far/I've settled for less & got much mo' than
I've expected...

                (Lights out...some men exit while other's remain on stage in the dark)

(   )

                ("I Had A Talk With God" is played in the background. Enters man wearing beige...
                the other men are sleeping, as the lights slowly emerges on stage. Man wearing beige
                gently wakes each one of the men & begins to tell them of the "Good News...")

God/
whispered in my ear this morning/
telling me/my child/wake up/for today is a new day/
& I have nothing but joy coming your way/

                (Woman enters and sits in a chair, centered stage...she starts reading;
                this inner prayer...**"After the earthquake came a fire, but the LORD**

was not in the fire. And after the fire came a gentle whisper."

I Kings 19:12—this is read in between each men's speech. . .like a call & response. . .)

for you see my child/
there will be no more hurt/no pain & most certainly no disappointments/
coming your way/

for/   (Enters man wearing black)
I am *Alpha* & *Omega*/
& I know all of your beginnings/
& I will most certainly be with you till the very end.../

my child wake up/   (Enters man wearing blue)
for joy cometh in the morning/& true peace is coming your way/

don't be starled/   (Enters man wearing yellow)
don't be afraid/for I have nothing but joy & peace coming your way/
wake up my child/   (Man wearing beige)
God/
whispered in my ear this morning.../
for there will be no mo' tears today/no sadness/no regrets/
& no passing of judgement/just joy & peace/
for your weary soul.../

for/   (Enters man wearing orange...)
I come/
to place a protective hedge of divide intervention/
around you & above you.../
as you seek comfort from within the hem of my garment.../

for/   (Enters man wearing green...)
I come to you in truth by way of eternal life/

for/   (Enters man wearing brown)
you shall no longer/
think of yourself as the denied stone/
but as a child of God/whom shall come forth as pure gold/

God/   (Man wearing beige)
whispered in my ear this morning/
telling me child sometimes...
you have asked the wrong people to pray for you!/

I tell you...now, my child/
to pray for yourself & remember:
for every season, there's a reason/for every no, there's a yes/
for every negative, I am the positive/for all your questions, I am the answer/
& for every one of your problems, I am the solution/
yes, be patient my child for I am God/

(Man wearing red walks over to man wearing beige & hugs him...they both start to weep)

be patient my child/
for I am God & I am just a prayer away/

have/   (Man wearing purple)
patience my child/
for I am God...& remember I am just a prayer away/

yes/   (Man wearing black)
God whispered in my ear this morning.../
yes/   (Man wearing red)
God whispered in my ear this morning.../

                    (Man wearing beige, as he slow embraces each man)

yes/
God whispered in my ear this morning.../

            Each man circles around the woman who is waiting with open arms)

yes/
God whispered in my ear this morning.../

            (Repeated by everyone to a very slow fade...as each person in slow motion &
                as if in a trance exits throughout the audience—laying on of hands—
                        letting the healing began...during curtain call,
                        "U Will Know" by Black Men United is played.)

FIN

Blackpoemology: Men of Colour in Transitory Stages-*Afterthought* (2001)

"June 5, 2001: News reported on the 20ᵗʰ Anniversary that HIV/AIDS has taken 22 million before their time, and that this is just the tip of the iceberg…and that African-American men between the ages of 23-29 are 14% infected reported daily within the 21ˢᵗ Century…

"A million didn't make it but I am one of the one's who did…(The Winans).

I am blessed to have had 22 million guardian angels watching over me!"

The year was 1998. **Two years** after my *"misdiagnosis"* of having contracted the HIV virus that can cause **AIDS,** only to find out that the diagnosis of having *"*KS*"* karposi sarcoma was true. **Four years** after Dr. David Ho was placed on the cover of *Time* magazine, naming him the *man-of-the-year* for discovering that *"*KS*"* can no longer be linked to [just] **HIV/AIDS** related illness but [maybe] considered a separate virus (*not necessarily sexual, but cancerous nevertheless*). **Eleven years** after <u>The New York Times</u> reported a rise in **HIV/AIDS** cases among African-American and Latino communities (*and only months since* [then] *President Bill Clinton declared a state of emergency on* **HIV/AIDS** *with the* <u>Black Caucus</u>. *I was still sitting in* **HIV/AIDS** *wards and injecting myself with Interform while attending work full time and attending graduate school*). No immediate help from the medical profession (for they had no clue as to what was the reason behind my having *"*KS*"* without **HIV** and or **AIDS**). **Two years** after my working through the *"meantime stages of a breakup,"* with a [then] potential soul-mate (*after six years together*). **Ten years** after the death of my estranged ex-spouse due to complications as a result of HIV/AIDS related illness. **Six years** after being exonerated from an *"alleged sexual assault of a minor in my care as a result of legal/societal red tape of the State of Georgia and the United States Armed Forces."* **Five years** after missing the transition into the hereafter of one out of three women in my life that made me feel whole and unconditionally loved (my God-mother Delores *"Tubby"* Lorde). **Four and Five years** of watching four of her son's succumb to their death as a result of HIV/AIDS related illness and or *"alleged"* suicide. **Eight years** after the birth of my one and only nephew—which, indirectly gave me (which Wm. Strayhorn had penned) *"Something to Live For (again)."* **Fourteen years** of loving and assisting my life-line-of-a-mother through her breast cancer treatments and surgery. **Twenty years** after deciding that I was not going to live a lie but be truthful to myself about myself (that in 1984), I had to go back on my word and revamp the living a lie journey…

in the Armed Forces (years before the *Don't Ask/Don't Tell* rhetoric). **Fifteen years** after writing "I wOnDeR sHoUlD I bE gRaTeFul '83, for **Blackheart's Journal**: *The Telling of Us All*, during my formative years at a writers workshop. Which was held at the former NYC Gay & Lesbian Center on West 13th Street. **One year** after writing the sequel to "I Wonder…" entitled "GOODBYE 2 the Last 4 Decades," I had woke up, hung over from drinking the night before and realized that my phone was turned off because I had missed a payment…REALITY CHECK!

Then all of a sudden, like a bolt of lighting, I realized that I needed help and woke up fast. For I was surely heading into a state of *"walking and functional depression"* (my own clinical term and not the doctors). The help came in the form of spirits and or guardian angels like: the numerous friends, family members and associates who have already lost their battles against HIV/AIDS, or the unknown angels like Langston, Strayhorn, Rustin and Baldwin and a host of others, who whispered in my ear that I had a story to tell, too! If not for others to understand or accept then to at least *"cleanse"* my soul and remove the stench of bitterness, pain and confusion. I was confusing love for lust. I was confusing external homophobias[ism], racism, sexism and class[ism] for (at times) internal homophobia[ism], racism, sexism and class[ism]. And, **twenty-two years** after seeing Ms. Ntozake Shange's *"for colored girls…"* on the **GREAT WHITE WAY**, I had finally attacked the man who had *"walked of with all my stuff"*…I had collected (in the case of Blackpoemology…) 87 poems, which tell the story of my journey's truth and exposed myself for the entire word to see!

Finally, I had completed my first attempt at playwrighting and immediately had it copyrighted. My next step was to photocopy 150+ copies in order for the "men (and *some women*)" in my life to validate it. It was disheartening that not all of them had embraced it. And for those that did I am indebted to (i.e., *Patrick Alford, Stewart Rutland, Earl Rodney-Holman, Patrick Lewis, Mr. & Mrs. Edwin Delegado, Deborah Hall and George "Jimmy" Harris, Melvin Smith, Derwin Keith Vega, Jean-Pierre Arcy, Kutcha and Steven G. Fullwood*, just to name a few)! For I had wished to see it performed on stage. But with the two hours and fifty minutes of allotted time frame—some had felt it was two long. Yet in my demonic state of mind, I had pointed out that **"Angels in America"** was in two parts and ran for several hours…but…I'll leave that alone…for now! Maybe you'll read about it in my memoirs…oh, what am I sayin' this is my memoir!

[Movin' right along] I will like to thank Steven G. Fullwood for assisting me in having the first manuscript placed in the Rare Books and Manuscript section of the NY Schomburg Library. And, last but of course far from least, I'd like to thank 1st Books Inc., Rich VanLue and staff for publishing my first collection of poems/prose as a choreopoem.

And, yes...I have finally accepted all of my blessing, for I am finally at a place in my life that I had never thought I'll be...healthy, much wiser and demon free! In closing, a question was beckoning to me by Damon J. Murphy, of Yahoo's Spirit of Black Gay Men regarding Bob Marley's "Redemptions Songs." He asked the following: "Who are the "Pirates" in your life? What are they selling you or have they sold you? How do we stop the bottomless pit? Are you working on freeing your mind? How long shall we watch our black gay prophets die? Are we fulfilling the books with our true story? Are we singing the songs of Freedom (redemption songs) or singing the songs of hatred with our oppressors?" I ask everyone reading this to come up with your own answers but remember our sons, brothers, uncles, cousin and fathers are still dying and until the black community, especially, wakes up to the devastion of HIV/AIDS in our own homes, "those Pirates," will once again raise their ugly heads.

david vincent brooks
Haarlem, New York
May/June 2001

A portion of proceeds that I,
david vincent brooks,
would receive directly or indirectly from this book
will go to the following organizations:

Gay Men of African Descent (**GMAD**)
103 East 125th Street, Suite 503
Haarlem, New York 10035

Life Force: Women Fighting AIDS Inc.,
175 Remsen Street, Suite 1100
Brooklyn Heights, New York 11201

Sexual Minority Alliance of Alameda County
(**SMAAC**) Youth Center
4058 13th Street, Box 263
Oakland, California 94612

In addition, I ask that all readers of "**BLACKPOEMOLOGY...**"
contact each one of the above organizations, with additional financial support
and/or personal request for additional information in either seeking
help for a loved one or for themselves...

In addition, I hope this inspires someone to become
more active in HIV/AIDS awareness and prevention,
and prevention of violence again men or women because
of their sexuality, ethnicity and or religion.

Peace, david

About the Author

David grew up in Bed-Stuy, Brooklyn and Rockaway Park, NYC. He is currently the Executive Producer of WBAI 99.5 (*Pacifica Foundations*) OUT FM, New York City's only L/G/T/Bi/2-spirited/ Inter-sexual communities radio program (serving all of NY, NJ, CT and parts of PA). He is a graduate of St. Francis College and plans on pursuing his Master's in Arts Administration come the year 2002. He has produced and directed two original plays, entitled: *Girl, Let Me Tell U*, in honor of Amanda Milan. Milan, a transgender person who was killed in NYC (June 2000), and *LOVERS THROUGHOUT THE AGES*, a musical. His latest project was directing *R.E.A.L.-Respect Every Aspect of Life*, by Haarlem's new playwright, Naima-Ali Thompson, with a group of talented young men and women. He has worked in Turkey, France and England during his ten years in the Armed Forces. An excerpt from this choreopoem will be featured in the forthcoming book, entitled *NO GUEST LIST!* by Qevin Oji, Grapevine Press Editor-in-Chief. David thanks all the men of Talk Safe, Gay Men of African Descent (GMAD), Gay Men's Health Crisis Center's Soul Food and HIV Arts Network for *"Putting up with hearing his stories, over and over and over again!"* This project is for the 22 million *"souls"* of HIV/AIDS legacy, as we enter the 21st year of this pandemic!

www.ingramcontent.com/pod-product-compliance
Lightning Source LLC
Chambersburg PA
CBHW020435290526
45785CB00002B/866